Birthday S[uite]

A Comedy

Robin Hawdon

Samuel French – London
New York - Sydney - Toronto - Hollywood

© 1984 BY ROBIN HAWDON PRODUCTIONS LTD

1. This play is fully protected under the Copyright Laws of the British Commonwealth of Nations, the United States of America and all countries of the Berne and Universal Copyright Conventions.

2. All rights, including Stage, Motion Picture, Radio, Television, Public Reading, and Translation into Foreign Languages, are strictly reserved.

3. No part of this publication may lawfully be reproduced in ANY form or by any means—photocopying, typescript, recording (including video-recording), manuscript, electronic, mechanical, or otherwise—or be transmitted or stored in a retrieval system, without prior permission.

4. Rights of Performance by Amateurs are controlled by SAMUEL FRENCH LTD, 52 FITZROY STREET, LONDON W1P 6JR, and they, or their authorized agents, issue licences to amateurs on payment of a fee. **It is an infringement of the Copyright to give any performance or public reading of the play before the fee has been paid and the licence issued.**

5. Licences are issued subject to the understanding that it shall be made clear in all advertising matter that the audience will witness an amateur performance; that the names of the authors of the plays shall be included on all announcements and on all programmes; and that the integrity of the author's work will be preserved.

The Royalty Fee indicated below is subject to contract and subject to variation at the sole discretion of Samuel French Ltd.

Basic fee for each and every
performance by amateurs   Code M
in the British Isles

In Theatres or Halls seating Six Hundred or more the fee will be subject to negotiation.

In Territories Overseas the fee quoted above may not apply. A fee will be quoted on application to our local authorized agent, or if there is no such agent, on application to Samuel French Ltd, London.

6. The Professional Rights in this play are controlled by SAMUEL FRENCH LTD.

The Professional Rights, other than Repertory Rights, in this play are controlled by RICHARD STONE, 18–20 York Buildings, Adelphi, London WC2N 6JU.

The publication of this play does not imply that it is necessarily available for performance by amateurs or professionals, either in the British Isles or Overseas. Amateurs and professionals considering a production are strongly advised in their own interests to apply to the appropriate agents for consent before starting rehearsals or booking a theatre or hall.

ISBN 0 573 11509 8

BIRTHDAY SUITE

First presented on a national tour in Autumn 1983 with the following cast of characters:

Tony	Brian Murphy
Bob	Trevor Bannister
Kate	Paula Wilcox
Dick	Derek Fowlds
Liz	Mary Maude

The action takes place in two adjoining bedrooms in a modern, medium-class, city hotel.

ACT I   Around 8 p.m.
ACT II   A few moments later

Time—the present

* TONY What's what?
BOB The lot!

ACT I*

Two adjoining hotel bedrooms. Around 8 p.m.

The two bedrooms, virtually identical but one a mirror-image of the other, are typical of a modern, medium-class, city hotel, with the maximum of comfort incorporated into the minimum of space. They are separated by a token "wall" down the centre of the stage with an inter-connecting door in the upstage section of it. In the back wall of each room is a main door out to the corridor. Upstage R and L in each room is a concealed double bed, which is lowered by hand from its alcove in the wall. (Note: only the bed in the L room is used—the other can be a dummy.) This whole upstage portion of each room could perhaps be on a stepped-up level from the downstage area. Downstage L and R are doors off to en suite bathrooms. There is also in each room a fitted clothes cupboard; a dressing-table unit with a mirror and stool; a drinks unit with a fridge and the usual array of miniature spirits bottles; a side-table and chairs which can be brought out for dining; armchairs, and a bedside table with a phone

When the CURTAIN *rises, the* R *room is arranged for a private dinner, with the bed concealed and the table and chairs set out for dinner in the centre of the room. The* L *room is arranged with the double bed concealed and the table and chairs set out of the way against the wall. An ice-bucket with a bottle of champagne is set in a prominent position*

The main door to the L *room opens and Tony, an Italian waiter, enters, followed by a distinctly apprehensive Bob, carrying a small overnight bag and wearing sunglasses*

Tony Here you are, sir. One of the nicest rooms in the hotel.
Bob Thank you. (*He takes off his sunglasses to inspect the room*)
Tony Make yourself comfortable. Bedroom here—bathroom there—wardrobe there—drinks there—
Bob (*looking around*) Isn't there something missing?
Tony No, sir. (*He lets the bed down*) It's there.
Bob Ah—clever. (*He indicates the connecting door*) What's that door there?
Tony That's not there.
Bob It's not?
Tony That's the door to next room when some filthy-rich Arab come to London and want a whole suite to himself. You don't wanna whole suite for what you wanna do, or do you?

---

*N.B. Paragraph 3 on page ii of this Acting Edition regarding photocopying and video-recording should be carefully read.

Bob No.
Tony That's what I thought. Now it's locked.
Bob I see.
Tony (*lifting up the champagne bucket with a flourish*) Bottla champagne—present from your friend Mr Tippett.
Bob (*muttering*) God, he goes too far.
Tony Anything else you want, you just call room-service and ask for Tony. Mr Tippett, he tell me I gotta look after you nice—understand?
Bob Yes—thank you.
Tony Your lady friend—she should be here in ten minutes or so. It's your birthday, yes?
Bob Yes.
Tony Ay, yi, yi—I wish I had friends give me birthday presents like that.

Bob nods unenthusiastically

   Whasa matter? You look nervous.
Bob I am.
Tony What for you nervous? This what life's all about.
Bob So they tell me.
Tony And I tell you something else. If this lady like mosta the ladies Mr Tippett bring here, then she a nice piece of pasta—you know what I mean?
Percival Does er—does Mr Tippett often bring ladies here then?
Tony Oh now and then. Lotta fellas bring a lotta ladies here. It's hard to remember them all.
Bob A real knocking shop, eh?
Tony A what?
Bob Nothing.
Tony It's a very respectable hotel, sir. But life gotta go on, you know what I mean?
Bob Yes.
Tony People don't realize—without half the hotels in the world, half the fellas in the world wouldn't be making love to half the chicks in the world—and that's a helluva lotta love short in the world.
Bob Quite a philosopher.
Tony Just because I'm a waiter don't mean I don't think. I see a lotta life here.
Bob I'm sure you do.
Tony OK. And remember, sir—anything you want, you ask for me, Tony.
Bob Thank you, Tony.
Tony You Bob, yes?
Bob (*nodding*) I'm Bob.

Tony holds out his hand for a tip

   (*Shaking Tony's hand*) How do you do.
Tony (*sourly*) I bring the lady up when she comes. Happy birthday, Bob!

Tony goes

Act I

Bob looks around him at a loss. He picks up the champagne bottle, looks at the label, puts it back in the bucket. It won't go right down because of all the ice. He makes several attempts, then jams the bottle down, causing several ice-cubes to fly out

Bob Oh God! (*He scurries about picking up the ice. He looks for somewhere to dry his hands. Finally he settles for the bedspread. Gingerly, he tests the bed. It is quite springy*) Oh God! (*He wanders to the dressing-table. He studies himself in the mirror*) Oh God! (*Despairingly, he smoothes his hair. He sits on the end of the bed looking very lost*)

The phone rings, making him jump. He puts his sunglasses on before answering

(*Answering it*) Hello? ... Oh, hello, Geoff. Yes I'm here. ... Yes, everything's fine, but ... Geoff, listen—I don't think I can go through with this. It's very good of you to fix it all up for me—but I mean ... well it's just not me, is it? Well I mean it's ridiculous—a man of my age—married twelve years—suddenly going wild and trying to—— Yes I know we've split up but I can't just start leading a wild bachelor life overnight. I'm a respectable civil servant, not an MP. ... Yes, but what if—what if I don't actually find—er—you haven't even told me her name. ... Mimi? Good Lord! What if I don't find Mimi very attractive? ... I'm sure she's superb, Geoff, but what I mean is, what if I can't actually—well, when it comes to it, what if I'm not able to actually ... (*Wearily*) Yes, Geoff, I'm sure she's very expert. With a name like Mimi, and a price like that, she'd have to be, wouldn't she? But that's what worries me—I'm not, you see, and I ... Yes, Geoff. ... All right, Geoff. ... OK, Geoff. ... Yes, Geoff. (*He replaces the receiver*) Oh God! (*He leaves the phone lying on the bed, heaves himself off the bed, goes to the champagne and contemplates the bottle for a moment. Then he wrinkles his nose and goes to the drinks. He opens a miniature bottle of Scotch and empties it into a glass. He has a good swig*)

He takes the glass and his bag into the bathroom and closes the door behind him

A moment's pause

The door of the R room opens from the corridor. Tony ushers in Kate, a girl of around thirty, very nervous, but determined not to show it

Tony Here you are, signorina. One of the nicest rooms in the hotel.
Kate Thank you. (*Looking round apprehensively*) There's no-one here.
Tony No, you're the first. Lemme take your coat.
Kate You mean he hasn't arrived yet?
Tony That's right.
Kate Oh dear, I er ...
Tony (*hanging the coat in the clothes cupboard*) Don't you worry—I expect he come any minute. I show him straight up. What's he look like?
Kate Er—well, I ... I'm not quite sure to tell you the truth.
Tony You don't know?

Kate No.
Tony Oh, I see—it's a business meeting.
Kate Well . . .
Tony When he ask for a special room for dinner, I think—well, you know—you wanna be private for other reasons. I'm sorry—my mistake. Course a lotta people meet a lotta people here for a lotta reasons—and a lotta people don't know what the other lotta people look like till after they've met them—you'd be surprised. But you're not one of those, I can tell.
Kate (*bewildered*) One of which?
Tony One of that lotta people. I see all of life come through here, signorina. I can tell what a person's here for just by looking at 'em.
Kate I'm sure you can.
Tony So what you here for?
Kate (*primly*) It's none of your business.
Tony Sorry, sorry. Anyway, you make yourself at home till your friend comes. Drinks over there—ice in the fridge. Here is your table for dinner. Soon as he here I bring you the menu.
Kate Thank you. (*Looking around*) Is there a bathroom?
Tony (*pointing*) Bathroom next door.

She hasn't seen him, and thinks he means the connecting door

Kate (*pointing to it*) Next door?
Tony (*busy checking the table setting*) That's right. Now—anything you want, you let me know. Tony's the name.
Kate Thank you, Tony.
Tony (*giving her a last appraising look from the door*) Business—ay, yi, yi, what a waste!

Tony goes

She stands for a moment

Kate Oh God! (*She looks at herself in the dressing-table mirror*) Oh God! (*She straightens her hair, and smooths an eyebrow. She goes to the drinks and pours herself a vodka and tonic. She has a sip, picks up her handbag, goes to the connecting door, opens it and enters the next room. She stops and stares at the bed*) Oh God! (*She hurriedly retreats back to her room and slams the door. She stands for a moment in thought, then peers into the other room again. Taking her handbag and glass with her, she nervously enters the other room, closing the connecting door behind her. She goes to the phone, puts her handbag and glass down on the bedside table, and dials, keeping a wary ear open for sounds next door*) Sally? It's me. He hasn't arrived yet. Sally, you'll never believe this. He's booked an entire suite! There's a room for dinner—that's fine—but there's also an adjoining bedroom! I swear it—I'm in there now. I'm actually sitting on the bed. And that's not all. He's got a bottle of champagne strategically placed *en route*! Sal, he's not a genuine lonely heart, he's just another male stud after an easy lay. He probably makes a regular thing of this. Works steadily through all the computer-dating agencies' lists in London. And his description on the list

Act I

they sent me is probably a total fiction. I mean, whoever heard of a psychiatrist going to something called "Soulmates Unlimited"? I expect he's got it to a fine art. Different date every night of the week, courtesy of IBM. Micro-chip sex! I'm just a sucker, Sal. I should have realized the moment he suggested a private room instead of a restaurant—I mean that's a dead givaway, isn't it? It's just that when he said he gets nervous in public places my heart went out to him, because that's exactly how I feel. What shall I do, Sal? He'll be here any minute. ... No, no I can't—it's too risky.

Bob appears in the bathroom doorway

I'm sure he's a—(*she breaks off as she sees Bob*)—very nice man. I'll call you later, Sal. (*She replaces the receiver and phone on the bedside table*)

Awkward pause

Bob Hello.
Kate Hello.
Bob You made it then?
Kate Yes, I er—I was just calling a friend. I didn't think you were here.
Bob I was just, er—just having a wash and brush-up.
Kate Ah. I didn't think you'd arrived.
Bob How did you get in?
Kate The room-waiter...
Bob Tony?
Kate That's right.
Bob Quite a character.
Kate He certainly is.

Pause

Bob Can I get you a drink?
Kate (*raising her glass*) I've already got one.
Bob Ah. (*He laughs nervously*) Made yourself at home.
Kate Yes.
Bob Good. There is champagne actually.
Kate I noticed.
Bob More of a spirits man myself, except on special occasions.
Kate Which I suppose this is.
Bob Well, for me. (*A nervous laugh*) Hardly for you.

Kate looks bemused

Must say, you're not quite what I expected.
Kate Aren't I?
Bob Not what I'd expect from old Geoff.
Kate Geoff?
Bob Yes, Geoff. At the office.
Kate Oh—at the office. I don't know him personally.
Bob (*puzzled*) Don't you?
Kate I did it all by correspondence.

Bob Really? I thought Geoff had picked you himself.
Kate He may have done. But the basic selection's all done by computer, isn't it?
Bob Is it really? Good God—even that now?
Kate Oh yes—they just feed in the basic facts and requirements, and out pop the names. To make sure you're well matched, you know.
Bob Amazing! Got everything to a fine art nowadays, haven't they? Sad really.
Kate Sad?
Bob So impersonal.
Kate I suppose so. But they've got to make the selection somehow.
Bob Yes.
Kate Didn't you know all that?
Bob Well I was rather under the impression that Geoff actually ... well, knew you intimate—— I mean personally, if you know what I mean.
Kate (*frowning*) I don't think so.
Bob It must be hard to remember them all.
Kate All?
Bob All the er—all the custom—— er, clients.
Kate The clients—oh yes, impossible.
Bob Of course.
Kate There are thousands.
Bob (*after a moment*) I suppose there are.
Kate Wouldn't be worth it otherwise, would it?
Bob No.

Pause

Kate You, er—obviously make a regular thing of this then.
Bob Me?
Kate You know whatsisname—Geoff so well.
Bob Oh yes, but we're just friends, that's all. I'm not like ... I mean, I don't ... I'm not used to this at all.
Kate I'm not sure I believe you.
Bob Why?
Kate Well—the champagne ...
Bob Oh that's Geoff's idea.
Kate Ah. And the bed.
Bob The bed?
Kate Yes.
Bob What about it?
Kate I didn't expect that.

Pause

Bob You didn't?
Kate A bit obvious, don't you think?
Bob (*staring at it*) I suppose it is.
Kate A bit unsubtle.
Bob Unsubtle? Oh, I see! You'd rather do without the bed?

Act I

Kate Well at this stage.
Bob You must forgive me. I'm not up with all the modern trends. I'm a bit old-fashioned about these things.
Kate Hardly seems that way to me.
Bob True, I assure you. I'm a very staid, very ordinary, very unambitious man, who's got involved in something that's a bit outside his scope. As a matter of fact, I was about to skip off before you arrived. I didn't think I could go through with it.
Kate Really?
Bob Yes.
Kate That's funny—so was I.

Pause

Bob So were you what?
Kate About to skip off.
Bob Why?
Kate Same reason as you.
Bob I don't quite follow.
Kate Well why were *you* so nervous about it?
Bob Because I've never done anything like this before.
Kate Neither have I.

Pause

Bob I mean, it's my first time.
Kate It's mine too.

Pause. Bob bursts into relieved laughter

Bob I see! I didn't understand! It's your first time!
Kate Yes.
Bob I *thought* you were a bit odd.
Kate Odd?
Bob Yes. I couldn't make you out at all. But *now* I get what Geoff's up to. He was highly secretive about it all, you see—just said you'd be right up my street. Crafty old devil! My God, he must have gone to some trouble to find *you*!
Kate Must he?
Bob (*looking at her in a new light*) Good heavens—your first time!
Kate (*a little annoyed*) Well do I look as if I'm a regular at it?
Bob No, you don't. That's what threw me. I naturally assumed you were, you see. (*Going to the drinks*) Have another drink.
Kate Thank you. Vodka and tonic.
Bob (*looking at her as he pours*) Your first time—Good Lord!
Kate (*awkwardly*) Well is it so surprising? Everyone has to start somewhere.
Bob I suppose so. It hadn't really occurred to me. (*Bringing her drink*) Tell me, why er ... what, er ... what made you go in for this sort of thing?
Kate We all get lonely, don't we?
Bob Well yes, but er—rather a drastic method, isn't it?
Kate Well why have you done it?

Bob Oh, dreams, fantasies—the frustrations of staid middle age.
Kae Does it have to be a fantasy?
Bob Well...
Kate Don't you think we might make a real relationship?
Bob (*with a sad laugh*) What an idealist you are. I don't imagine you'll stay that way for long.
Kate (*angrily*) Well for heaven's sake, what do you suppose is the whole purpose of this exercise? Shake hands, have a quick drink, and then into bed? Wham, bam, thank you ma'am, and then go our separate ways? Eh?

Pause

Bob Well—yes.
Kate Well thank you!

She throws her drink in his face, and storms through to the other room, slamming the door. He sits, stunned, his face dripping, staring at the connecting door

Bob Good Lord! Thank God I didn't give her ice! (*He mops his face with his handkerchief, and goes to the connecting door. He opens it gingerly, and peers in*)

Kate is sitting in the armchair with her back to him

  This door's open!
Kate Of course it's open. How do you expect to get through it unless it's open?
Bob I thought that... (*He sees the dinner-table*) It's set for dinner.
Kate Well didn't you order dinner?
Bob I don't know—I left everything to Geoff.
All Who is this Geoff—your nursemaid?
Bob I don't quite understand. There's something wrong here.
Kate You bet there's something wrong. You're after a cheap lay, and you thought I'd jump at the chance just because I'd signed on at the agency.
Bob Agency?
Kate You might think that because of that I'm so desperate for a bit of sex I'd find you irresistible, but I've got news for you. You're not.
Bob No, no—I don't think that at all. I was under the impression that you were...
Kate What?
Bob Er... (*He looks towards the other room and then back, trying to work it out*) Can I ask you something? Did Tony show you into that room or this one?
Kate This one of course. I'd have run a mile if that bed had been the first thing I'd seen.
Bob I think there's been a mistake.
Kate You bet there has.
Bob I don't think I'm the person you think I am.
Kate Well I'm certainly not the person you think *I* am!
Bob No, I don't think you are.

Act I 9

Kate I'm glad we've got that straight. Now will you please go back to your champagne and your bed, and leave me alone.

She sniffs loudly and rummages for her handkerchief. He comes to her and gingerly touches her shoulder

Bob Please, don't cry. I——
Kate Go away!
Bob I didn't mean all those——
Kate Go *away*!
Bob Right. (*He goes to the door, then turns*) Er ...
Kate What?
Bob *You* won't go away, will you?
Kate Go *away*!
Bob Right.

He retreats into the other room. She sobs uncontrollably into her handkerchief

Kate Oh damn, damn, damn!
Bob (*walking up and down next door*) Damn, damn, damn! (*He stops*) Agency ... I get it! (*He has a swig of whisky and stands thinking*) Come on, Robert my lad—this is what you've been waiting for all your life. What are you going to do about it? (*He raps his forehead*) Think!

There is a knock and Tony enters the L room with a menu

Tony Shall I bring you the menu, sir? Maybe you like dinner first.
Bob First? Oh, er ... thank you. (*He takes it*) Dinner—that's it!
Tony Eh?
Bob Tony, has there been any sign of my, er—lady friend yet?
Tony No, sir.
Bob I thought not.
Tony Don't worry—she'll come.
Bob And next door—the lady there. Who is *she* expecting can you tell me?
Tony How you know about the lady next door?
Bob I've met her, that's how.
Tony You met her?
Bob Yes.
Tony (*pointing towards the corridor*) Outside?
Bob No, in here.
Tony How she get in here?
Bob (*pointing*) Through the door.
Tony Through that door?
Bob Yes.
Tony It's locked.
Bob It's not locked.
Tony I locked it myself.
Bob It's not locked.
Tony I tell you it's locked! (*He tries the door, it opens. He closes it again*) It's not locked.
Bob No.

Tony (*fiddling with the key*) The lock—it's jammed.
Bob Listen, Tony—how would you like to earn yourself ten pounds? (*He gets out his wallet*)
Tony (*still fiddling*) I don't think I can do this. I think it's... (*He straightens up*) Ten pounds?
Bob Yes.
Tony (*warily*) A nice gentleman like you, giving a lotta money like that—that's gotta be dangerous. I been in this job a long time. I like it here. I don't take bribes—it's a principle with me.
Bob Oh, I'm sorry. (*He puts his wallet away*)
Tony I'll do it—what you want?
Bob Well, that lady is expecting a gentleman for dinner—right?
Tony Right.
Bob I'd like to have dinner with her instead.
Tony How you gonna do that?
Bob I don't know, but I'd like to try.
Tony She a nice lady.
Bob Yes, she is. Much more my type than the other one.
Tony How you know? You haven't met the other one yet. She one of Mr Tippett's ladies, then she a real cracker.
Bob That's what I mean. I'm not really into real crackers—especially when they're called Mimi.
Tony That her name—Mimi?
Bob Yes.
Tony Mama!
Bob And you see, I'm just not a Mama—er, Mimi sort.
Tony No—you don't look that sort.
Bob But that lady next door—that's something quite different. I haven't met anyone quite as nice as that in years. And you see, she doesn't know the man who's supposed to be meeting her here, does she?
Tony That's right. It's business.
Bob How do you know it's business?
Tony What else could it be if she don't know him? A lady like that doesn't do Mimi-type business—she does business-type business.
Bob I don't think it's any-type business. I think it's an arranged meeting. Through one of those computer-dating agencies—you know?
Tony Ah—one of those. Pot-luck job, huh?
Bob You could put it that way. But that means it doesn't really matter whether she has dinner with him or with me, does it?
Tony I see what you mean. You're quite a crafty operator. So what about the other guy when he arrives?
Bob Well that's where you come in. If you can manage to make him happy with *my* lady, then it's worth ten pounds to you.
Tony How can I do that?
Bob Look—if she's as attractive as you say she will be, and he's so much in need he has to go to an agency...
Tony Aha—I see what you mean. He's looking for a can of spaghetti, and she's offering a supermarket.

Bob Something like that.
Tony So—you gonna have dinner in there with that lady ...?
Bob That's the plan.
Tony And he gonna be in here with the other lady? Seems to me you making for a dangerous situation.
Bob More than likely.
Tony Didn't your friend Geoff tell me you a married man?
Bob That's right.
Tony Mama mia—you making for a *helluva* dangerous situation!
Bob Tony, I'm a very dull and boring chap, who's led a very dull and boring existence for far too long, and if I don't take this chance for a bit of danger now, then I'll regret it for the rest of my life.
Tony Sure—I get you. I like that. I just hope the danger isn't too dangerous. OK—I'll do it.
Bob Thank you.
Tony (*putting his hand out*) Five pound up front. Danger money.
Bob (*giving him a fiver*) There you are. Now you'd better get down to reception quickly—they'll both be here any minute. I'm going next door.
Tony OK. (*He starts to go*)
Bob And take our orders for dinner in there as soon as you can.
Tony OK. (*He starts to go again*)
Bob You'd better put that bed away before they come.
Tony Yes, sir. (*He lifts the bed back into the wall*)
Bob And fix that lock when I'm on the other side.
Tony I can tell this is gonna be a busy evening.

Tony goes

Bob smooths his hair and prepares to go next door. Just as he is about to go through the connecting door he remembers something

Bob My bag!

He looks around, remembers where he put it and hurries into the bathroom. While he is there the door to the corridor opens and Tony sticks his head in again. He looks about, sees the coast is apparently clear, and opens the door wide

Tony (*talking back into the corridor*) It's a good job I catch you, sir. You about to go in the wrong room.

Bob comes back out of the bathroom, sees Tony and freezes

This your room. One of the nicest rooms in the hotel.

Panic-stricken, Bob vanishes back into the bathroom with his overnight bag. Dick appears from the corridor and enters. He carries a furled umbrella and is making a good pretence of being extremely cool

Dick (*looking round*) Ah yes, yes, yes. (*Pointing at the drinks*) Ah—good, good. (*He goes and feels the "curtains"*) Fine, fine. (*Opening the clothes cupboard*) Bathroom?

Tony No, sir—wardrobe.
Dick (*emerging again*) Ah yes—good, good. (*He sees the connecting door*) Ah—bathroom there.
Tony No, sir—that's locked. (*He opens the bathroom door*) Bathroom there.
Dick Ah, splendid, splendid. Toilet too?
Tony Yes, sir—we think of everything. (*He goes to the bed and lets it down*)

Dick starts

Dick Er—what's that?
Tony Whassit look like?
Dick It's a bed.
Tony Right first time.
Dick Yes, but er—I didn't ask for a bed. (*He prods it with his umbrella*)
Tony Don't worry, sir—you don't wanna bed, you don't have a bed.

He lifts it up into its alcove, trapping Dick's umbrella between the bed and the wall

See—sparito!
Dick Er—I seem to have er . . .
Tony (*releasing the umbrella*) Sorry, sir.
Dick Fine, fine. (*He sees the champagne and lifts it out of the bucket*) What's this?
Tony (*studying it earnestly*) After-shave?
Dick I mean what's it doing here? I didn't order champagne.
Tony (*replacing it*) Champagne on the house, sir. We like to make a new customer feel at home.
Dick Your profit margins must be very slim. Er—where do we eat dinner—on the floor?
Tony (*bringing out the side-table*) Don't you worry—we got all mod cons here.
Dick Well that's fine, fine. But what I don't understand is, er . . .
Tony What, sir?
Dick Why isn't the lady here yet? I got held up, but she should be here.
Tony Listen, sir—I gotta tell you something.
Dick What's that?
Tony It's not the lady you're expecting.
Dick What do you mean?
Tony It's a different lady. The first lady—she send a message saying she change her mind, she not coming. But she send a friend instead.
Dick A friend?
Tony Yes—a real cracker.
Dick Cracker?
Tony I mean a real nice lady. A lady you like very much.
Dick I don't want another lady. I want that lady.
Tony This a real special lady, sir.
Dick I want that special lady. I chose her from hundreds.
Tony You know hundreds of ladies?
Dick Well, er . . .

Act I

Tony You a lucky man.
Dick You don't understand. I particularly want that lady and that lady alone. I went to a great deal of trouble to find someone who suited my needs.
Tony (*winking*) Ah—I understand.
Dick You *don't* understand. She was chosen very specifically from a long list, and——
Tony What she look like?
Dick I don't know.
Tony Aha, I understand.
Dick You *don't* understand! This is a special introduction. A very charming, respectable girl who likes cats, antiques and country walking.
Tony Sounds dynamite to me. Nobody's that simple.
Dick (*angrily*) Look, what business is it of yours anyway?
Tony Sorry, sir. But they all the same underneath. You take a tip from Tony—I know.
Dick Yes, I've no doubt you do.
Tony Now this chick that's coming instead, she a real nice piece of pasta.
Dick Pasta?
Tony Yes, sir—she just what any man would like. No problems, no demands. She give you what you want, she leave you when you want, she make you a happy man.
Dick How do you know what she's like?
Tony The other lady tell me.
Dick (*puzzled*) I don't understand. She didn't seem the sort to send along a deputy. What does she do?
Tony Anything you like.
Dick I mean, what is her job?
Tony Ah. Er—I don't know, sir. But I know she's a very nice girl. Her name is Mimi.
Dick Mimi?
Tony Yes—nice name.
Dick (*nodding*) For a French poodle. No, no, it won't do. I'm leaving.
Tony (*barring his way*) Hold on, sir. You can't go now. What a waste of a lady. She's paid for too.
Dick Paid for?
Tony I mean, she paid for her fare to get here.
Dick She's *not* here.
Tony She will be any minute. It's not fair on her, sir. She come all this way to keep you happy, and you run out on her before you even met her.
Dick Where *has* she come from?
Tony Round the corner, sir. Er—round the corner from where the other lady was gonna come from.
Dick Kew?
Tony No, sir—you're the first. Oh, I see—yes, that's right.
Dick (*wavering*) Well I must say, it's the most extraordinary arrangement I've ever heard of.
Tony Don't worry—it all work out, I promise. Now you go and have a nice

wash, brush-up. Tony get everything ready for dinner, OK? You may as well meet her at least—if only to say goodbye.
Dick Well all right—but if she's not here by the time I come out again I'm leaving, understand?
Tony Sure, sir, I——

Bob sticks his head out of the bathroom door and frantically signals to Tony behind Dick's back

Ahhh!

Dick, who is turning towards the bathroom, jumps and turns back

Dick What's the matter?
Tony (*desperately improvising*) Ah—I er ... I forgot to show you the fridge, sir.

He practically frogmarches Dick to the fridge

It's a wonderful fridge, sir. Look at that ice-compartment.

He forces Dick's head down almost into the fridge

All the ice you want night or day.

He waves to Bob who drops on to his hands and knees and crawls upstage towards the connecting door, dragging his overnight bag with him

Dick (*straightening up*) What on earth are you talking about? I'm not interested in ice-boxes!
Tony No?

Bob has lost his overnight bag. He tries to return for it, but is forced to carry on crawling as Dick turns away from the fridge. Tony grabs Dick by the shoulders and turns him so as to keep his back to Bob

Sorry, sir, I thought you like to see it. I thought you be interested.

Bob gets to the connecting door, reaches up to the handle and opens it

Dick What the hell for? What are you talking about?
Tony (*leading Dick at the double across to the bathroom*) Never mind, sir— have a look at the bathroom. That's *really* worth seeing!
Dick You're mad!

Tony pushes Dick into the bathroom

Tony (*seeing Bob's bag*) Here, sir—you forgot your bag. (*He throws the bag into the bathroom*)
Bob (*hissing frantically*) No!

Too late—Tony slams the bathroom door and waves furiously at Bob to get out. Bob does so closing the connecting door behind him. Bob and Tony collapse against their respective door-posts and regain their breath. Kate looks round

Kate I thought I told you to leave me alone.
Bob (*breathlessly*) Sorry, I ...
Kate What's the matter?

Act I   15

Bob I just had rather a tricky journey getting here.
Kate (*bemused*) What?

Next door, Tony goes out to the corridor

Bob (*recovering his composure*) Look, do you think we could possibly start again?
Kate Why?
Bob I'm afraid I got off on the wrong foot.

No answer

It was clumsy of me to jump in with both feet like that.

No answer

I'm sorry if I put my foot in it.
Kate What are you—a centipede?
Bob I'd got it all wrong you see.
Kate I think you had. Yet you sounded so gentlemanly on the phone.
Bob Did I?
Kate Almost prudish.
Bob Oh I am, I am.
Kate Tell me, I'm interested—what gave you the impression that—well that was all I wanted from this meeting?
Bob Well, I er . . .
Kate Was it this Geoff character?
Bob Yes, that's right. It was his fault.
Kate I don't understand. I don't know anyone at the office. I'm sure he doesn't know me.
Bob He must have been confusing you with someone else.
Kate But you had all my details on your list. Boutique manageress—likes cats, antiques and country walking. Doesn't sound much like rampant nymphomaniac, does it?
Bob No—certainly not.
Kate So why the bed and the champagne?
Bob Forget them. Put them out of your mind. I've told Tony to have this door locked.
Kate But why—that's what I can't understand? Why such a crude approach? Is that what they teach you at the Royal College of Psychiatrists?
Bob Psychiatrists?
Kate Yes. I wouldn't have thought a career like that was an inducement to wild profligacy. Or does Freud really get to you in the end?
Bob Certainly not.
Kate I was so looking forward to discussing all that with you too. I've never known a real psychiatrist.
Bob Oh dear. This isn't going to be as easy as I'd hoped.
Kate You're dead right it's not.
Bob No, not that—I mean, er . . . Look, let's change the subject. Let's talk about you. Tell me all about yourself.
Kate Vital measurements?

Bob No, no. I want to get the feel of you—no, I don't. I mean I want to know what you're like underneath.
Kate You want me to lie on the couch for you?
Bob No, no—I want to know who you are. For instance, how come you got into clothes? Oh my God, this is getting worse and worse!
Kate (*laughing*) I'll let that one go. Well you see, I have this very old friend called Sally who opened a boutique. It was doing so well that one day she just thought, "I know—I'll ask Kate if she'd like to manage the shop for me".
Bob Who's Kate?

Slight pause

Kate Me.
Bob Oh. Oh, I see! Kate—yes of course, silly of me. Kate, yes—I'd got used to thinking of you as Katherine, you see.
Kate Why? Nobody calls me Katherine.
Bob Don't they?
Kate No.
Bob Isn't that what it said on your form?
Kate No, Kate.
Bob Funny. I must have just assumed that. I always think of Kates as Katherines—ever since seeing *Taming of the Shrew*.
Kate Ah. You identified me with the shrew.
Bob No, no—not at all. Just the association of names—you know. "Come, kiss me Kate, and . . ." No, that's not right either. (*He sighs*) Oh Lord, I'm not doing this very well.
Kate You're terribly nervous, aren't you? Wavering between a blatant Casanova and tongue-tied adolescent. You're not a schizophrenic, are you?
Bob Perhaps that's it. Do you think I should see a shrink?
Kate You are a shrink.
Bob So I am. (*A feeble laugh*) Cliché'd professional joke.
Kate I don't know why I'm sitting here listening to all this nonsense. I should have walked out at the start.

Slight pause

Bob You didn't though.
Kate What?
Bob You could have walked out, but you didn't. (*After a pause*) Why didn't you?
Kate I don't know. I suppose . . .
Bob What?
Kate Having gone through such agony forcing myself to come here, I was loathe to see it all melt away to nothing. All because of that stupid bed.
Bob Forget the bed.
Kate And I suppose I felt . . . that underneath you weren't really like that.
Bob I'm not.
Kate Despite the champagne.

Act I

Bob Forget the champagne.
Kate And I suppose I felt ... I quite like champagne ...
Bob Do you?
Kate And beds ...
Bob Ah.
Kate But in the right place, and at the right time.
Bob Quite.
Kate Not the very second you've just shaken hands.
Bob No.
Kate Incidentally, we didn't.
Bob That's right, we didn't. (*He holds out his hand*) Hello, Kate.
Kate (*taking it*) Hello, Dick.
Bob (*looking behind him*) Where? Who? Dick? (*He realizes*) Oh yes—Dick! (*He laughs*) How d'you do.
Kate What's the matter with you?
Bob Er—Richard. I prefer to be called Richard.
Kate You signed yourself Dick.
Bob Yes. I use Dick as a professional persona. The real me is Richard.
Kate You really *are* a schizophrenic.
Bob I'm rapidly heading that way, yes.
Kate I should have left. I don't know what I'm getting myself into here.
Bob No please, don't leave. At least have dinner with me.
Kate With both of you at once?
Bob With whichever one you'd like.
Kate I'll tell you what.
Bob What?
Kate I'll go into the bathroom and tidy myself up a bit. You decide amongst the two of you which one you'd like me to meet. And then I'll come out and we'll start afresh. How's that?
Bob That's a splendid idea.
Kate Right. (*She rises and heads for the connecting door*)
Bob No!

She stops

Er—not in there. Wrong associations.
Kate Well where?

He looks around, and sees the other bathroom door

Bob Oh look. (*He opens it*) There's another bathroom here. How's that?
Kate Awful lot of bathrooms in this hotel.
Bob Caters for very clean people.
Kate Or very dirty ones. See one of you later.

She goes into the bathroom

Bob is at a bit of a loss

Bob Well, Bob fella ... Dick fella ... whoever you are fella ... you've got your hands full this evening! (*He gets himself a drink and sits in the armchair*)

Tony enters the L room, carrying cutlery
He listens at the bathroom door for a moment, then busies himself laying the table for dinner and uncorking the champagne

Liz appears in the main doorway behind him. She carries a note in one hand, and looks somewhat put-out

Tony surreptitiously samples some of the champagne

Liz Good-evening.

Tony jumps and spews champagne into the air

Tony *(recovering)* Ah—good-evening, signora. Come in. The gentleman's expecting you. He's in the bathroom.
Liz He's expecting me in the bathroom?
Tony No, no. Not right now anyway. He be out subito.
Liz I see.
Tony Lemme take your coat.
Liz *(coolly)* Not just yet, thank you.
Tony Why? You gonna wear your coat all night?
Liz I haven't decided that I'm staying yet.
Tony What you mean? Mr Tippett, he ask you to come, yes?
Liz *(nodding towards the bathroom)* Yes, but that's not Mr Tippett, is it?
Tony So what's it matter to you who it is?
Liz It matters quite a lot who it is. I'm very choosy when it comes to my partners for the evening.
Tony Ay, yi, yi—I must say you not like mosta Mr Tippett's chicks. They got class, but you got *real* class!
Liz You know Mr Tippett I gather?
Tony Sure—he and I old friends. I look after him a lot here. He's a hot one for the ladies.
Liz So I believe.
Tony But you the hottest one yet. *(He taps on the bathroom door)* The lady here, sir—and how!
Dick *(off, muffled)* Oh, er—won't be a moment.
Tony OK, signorina. Now you gonna give him a real nice evening, yes?
Liz I was under the impression *I* was to have the real nice evening.
Tony You do everything right, you *both* have a real nice evening. That's what life's all about. *(Indicating)* Now—champagne when you want it—dinner for two when you want it—and when you want it ... *(He pulls out the bed a foot or two)* Presto!
Liz *(with eyes narrowed)* Very neat. Was the bed Geoff Tippett's idea?
Tony No, that's the architect's idea. Geoff Tippett just pay for it.
Liz Did he indeed?
Tony Wassit matter anyway? All you need to know is if you're gonna go to bed there's a bed to go to bed in. And one other thing.
Liz Yes?
Tony Er—how can I put this ...? Don't be surprised if the gentleman turns out to be not quite the gentleman you're expecting.
Liz I won't.

Act I

Tony (*surprised*) You won't?
Liz I'd already gathered that.
Tony You're a very smart lady. (*Relieved*) Well that's fine—so you just get on and do your job and don't ask any question, OK?
Liz Listen, my friend—you just get on and do *your* job and leave me to look after mine, right?
Tony That's what I'm saying.
Liz Fine.
Tony So take your coat off.
Liz (*angrily*) I'll take my coat off when I'm good and ready!
Tony OK, OK, OK! Mama mia—I don't know what makes a sophisticated chick like you go in for a game like this. I tell you, I see a lotta life in this job and I always get new surprises.
Liz I know the feeling.
Tony I bring you the menu for dinner soon. Arrivederci—Mimi!

Tony goes

Liz looks around speculatively. She sees Kate's handbag by the phone on the bedside table and inspects it curiously. Then she looks pensively at the note in her hand and sits in the armchair. There is a knock on the R room door

Bob Come in.

Tony sticks his head in

Tony It's going good, sir?
Bob Yes, thank you.
Tony Where the lady?
Bob (*nodding towards the bathroom*) Touching up her make-up.
Tony Aha. It's going *very* good.
Bob I'm not sure.
Tony Sure it is. When a lady put on her make-up at the start of an evening, it mean she ready to take off everything else at the end—know what I mean?
Bob You're so subtle, Tony.
Tony Sure—I see all of life here.
Bob So you keep saying.
Tony I bring you the menu for dinner, yes?
Bob Yes, please.
Tony Oh, and by the way—everything going good next door too.
Bob Oh fine. Is she at the stage of putting on her make-up, or taking off everything else?
Tony Ha, ha—I bring you progress report later. And I tell you this too— you could be making a big mistake.
Bob Why?
Tony She one helluva birthday present!

Tony goes

Bob contemplates his drink again, then during the following gets up and wanders over to the table

In the L room the bathroom door opens and Dick comes hesitantly out Dick and Liz stare at each other

Dick Hello.
Liz Hello.
Dick Nice of you to come.
Liz Not at all.
Dick Splendid, splendid. Er ... got here all right then?
Liz Yes.
Dick It's tricky.
Liz What is?
Dick Kew.
Liz Q?
Dick Yes.
Liz Letter, billiards, or bus?
Dick I beg your pardon?
Liz Which kind of Q?
Dick The place Kew.
Liz Oh. What's tricky about it?
Dick Getting there.
Liz From where?
Dick Here.
Liz Is it?
Dick Isn't it?
Liz I suppose it is.

Pause. Both stand flummoxed

I must say this isn't quite what I was expecting.
Dick Isn't it?
Liz No.
Dick Well it's not what I was expecting either. But then I expected that.
Liz I beg your pardon?
Dick Come to think of it, it's not quite what I expected even after not getting what I expected in the first place.
Liz Do you mind telling me what you're talking about?
Dick I mean you don't quite fit the description, "a nice piece of pasta". (*Hastily*) Though I'm very glad.
Liz So am I.
Dick Anyway, thank you for coming. (*He holds out his hand*) I'm Dick.
Liz (*frowning*) I thought you were Tony.
Dick No, Dick.
Liz This is getting more and more confusing.
Dick You're Mimi?
Liz No, I'm Liz.
Dick (*frowning*) Yes, it is confusing, isn't it?
Liz I take it you were expecting to meet someone called Mimi?
Dick No—someone called Kate.
Liz Ah.

Act I

Dick And you were expecting to meet someone called Tony?
Liz No—someone called Geoff.
Dick Ah. (*After a pause*) I think I'm going mad.
Liz Let's start again, shall we?
Dick Right.
Liz (*slowly and carefully*) You came here, having arranged to meet a Kate?
Dick Right.
Liz For dinner?
Dick Yes.
Liz But she's not here?
Dick No. I was told to expect a Mimi instead.
Liz Who told you?
Dick Tony.
Liz Ah. So there *is* a Tony.
Dick He's the waiter.
Liz The waiter. (*After a pause*) How odd.
Dick And you had arranged to meet a Geoff for dinner?
Liz Yes.
Dick And you were told to expect a Tony instead.
Liz That's right.
Dick Who told *you*?
Liz (*holding up the note*) This note. It was waiting for me at reception. (*Reading*) "Sorry, can't make it. But Tony will look after you. Have a lovely evening. Geoff."
Dick Ah—that explains the Tony bit. He meant Tony will serve you. But why here? Are you sure you've got the right room?
Liz Yes. It's booked in Geoff's name.
Dick Is it? I thought it was booked in mine.
Liz Did you see that in the register?
Dick No, but Tony met me outside and brought me in here. He seemed quite certain.
Liz Do you suppose he thought you were Geoff?
Dick I told him who I was.
Liz I wonder where Geoff's got to then?
Dick Well he's certainly *been* here.
Liz How do you know?
Dick Somebody has. There's a man's overnight bag in the bathroom.
Liz That's odd. There's a woman's handbag over there.
Dick Good Lord!
Liz Do you suppose it's Kate's or Mimi's?
Dick This could turn into quite a party.
Liz (*taking off her coat*) Well, while we're waiting for it to start, why don't we have a drop of that champagne?
Dick I suppose we could. It's on the house.
Liz It's on Geoff actually—but it doesn't really matter.
Dick Er—who *is* Geoff—or is it rude of me to ask?
Liz He's a friend of mine—or rather of Bob's.
Dick (*nervously*) There's a Bob as well?

Liz My husband.
Dick Ah. Is he coming too?
Liz No. You see, er—well it's rather an involved story.
Dick I'll tell you mine if you'll tell me yours.
Liz My marriage is on the rocks.
Dick Ah—I know what it's like.
Liz Are you in the same boat?
Dick My boat went down three years ago.
Liz I'm sorry.
Dick Oh it can be quite fun in the water. (*He hands her a glass of champagne*) Try it.
Liz Thank you. Well, you see, I'm married to a civil servant. A nice man—terribly nice—but oh so dull! He's the sort of man who polishes the cutlery on his tie in restaurants . . .

Next door, Bob is absent-mindedly doing just that

. . . who crumbles saccharin tablets on to strawberries and cream . . .

Bob is fishing in his pockets. He pulls out a box of saccharin tablets, rattles it, puts it back and goes on searching through his pockets

. . . who buys his cigarettes in tens and wonders why he's always running out.

Bob has found what he is looking for—a packet of ten cigarettes. It is empty

Bob mutters to himself and hurries out of the room

Dick How interesting.
Liz What's interesting about it?
Dick I'm a psychiatrist. I find that sort of behaviour fascinating.
Liz Well I'm a wife and I find it infuriating!
Dick Where is he now?
Liz On a business trip to Manchester.
Dick How long?
Liz For ever as far as I know. We had a row over what I was getting him for his birthday and he stormed off saying he wasn't coming back.
Dick What *were* you getting him?
Liz A pair of gardening gloves.
Dick I can see why he left.
Liz Yes, but I didn't always give him things like that. (*She starts to sniff*) I once bought him a very trendy jogging suit. He used it as pyjamas. I once gave him a pair of Gucci crocodile shoes. He wore them for golf. (*In floods of tears*) I gave up.
Dick (*in a panic*) Oh look here, please don't cry! Please, don't do that! Look, have some more . . . (*He grabs the napkin round the champagne bottle, but only succeeds in pulling over the ice-bucket. Ice falls all over the floor*) Oh dear, I . . . (*He goes down on his hands and knees to pick it up*)
Liz (*drying her eyes*) Did you say you were a psychiatrist?
Dick Yes.

Liz What do you do with distraught patients—have a nervous breakdown yourself?
Dick Well, believe it or not, I'm very good in the consulting room.
Liz What's the difference?
Dick Those are clients. You're a real person.
Liz It's a wonder you have any clients left.
Dick I'm a very good psychiatrist actually. I'm just hopeless at my own relationships. I've already been through one disastrous marriage, and now I'm looking round for another one. I can't live with anyone, you see—and I can't live without anyone either. I'm a mess.
Liz You sound just like a normal man to me.
Dick I eventually got so lonely that ... You promise not to laugh?
Liz I promise.
Dick Well, I contacted one of those computer-dating agencies—"Soulmates Unlimited".

Liz covers up an involuntary splutter

You promised!

She controls herself

Through them I ... well, to cut a long story short, I arranged to meet someone for a quiet private dinner here.
Liz Kate?
Dick Yes. But then I was delayed ... well, no I wasn't. To tell you the honest truth, it took me twenty minutes to pluck up the courage to enter the hotel. But when I finally arrived here, Tony told me that she'd changed her mind and was sending along a friend instead.
Liz Mimi?
Dick Yes. Which is who I assumed you were.
Liz I see.
Dick Amazing, isn't it? You go through all that trouble to have your most crucial psychological needs matched by computerized selection from thousands of people and you end up drinking champagne with someone you have no connection with whatsoever. (*He tops up her glass*) Have some more.
Liz Thank you. I'm sorry your Kate didn't turn up.
Dick I'm not. Anyone as perfect as she seemed to be on paper would be sure to turn out disastrous in the flesh.
Liz Do you mean that literally?
Dick What do you mean?
Liz Were you expecting to get as far as lowering that bed on the first evening?
Dick Good heavens, no! I was appalled when I saw that. I just expected a quiet intimate room for dinner.
Liz So did I. I wonder what's going on.
Dick I'm not sure that I mind very much.
Liz What do you mean?
Dick I'm quite enjoying myself. Is your marriage really finished?

Liz Definitely.
Dick Good—I mean terrible.
Liz You mean good. I'm going to *live* a bit from now on.
Dick Me too. (*Pouring champagne*) Let's start tonight.
Liz Why not?
Dick (*raising his glass*) Here's to Geoff. Long may he stay away.
Liz And here's to Kate and Mimi—let's hope they're both stuck in Kew.

They clink glasses. There is a knock at the L main door

   Tony enters, carrying two menus

Dick Ah, here's the cue—I mean the key.
Liz Yes, I think he is.
Tony The dinner menu, sir.
Dick Thank you.
Tony Everything going good?
Liz Everything going very good, thank you.
Tony Good.

He holds out the menu which she does not immediately take

Liz You're Tony?
Tony Si, signorina.
Liz Well, Tony, before we get around to dinner, would you by any chance know why Mr Tippett isn't here this evening?
Tony (*warily*) Mr Tippett?
Liz Yes.
Tony You know why he not here.
Liz Do I?
Tony Sure you do.
Liz I thought I was supposed to be having dinner with him.
Tony Not with him.
Liz Then with who?
Tony (*indicating Dick*) With him.
Liz No, not with him.
Tony Yes, with him.
Liz No, *not* with him!
Tony Then with who?
Liz That's what I'm asking you.
Tony Don't ask me—I'm just the waiter.
Liz You seem to know better than anyone what we're all doing here tonight.
Tony (*in a fierce whisper*) I told you—you here to do your stuff and ask no questions!
Liz (*dangerously*) No, Tony—I always ask questions before I do my stuff. And you'd better give me some answers before I do you. (*Slowly and deliberately*) Now, let's start again. Where's the lady who's supposed to be meeting this gentleman?
Tony (*nervously*) You're the lady.
Liz No, Tony—try again.

Act I

Tony The first lady—she couldn't come. I told him.
Dick And what about the second lady?
Tony (*indicating Liz*) She the second lady.
Liz No, I'm the third lady.
Tony (*wide-eyed*) You mean there's another lady?
Liz It would seem so.
Tony Ay, yi, yi—this getting out of control.
Liz It will do if they all turn up at once. Now are you quite sure we're both in the right room?
Tony (*emphatically*) Absolutely! Sure it's the right room!
Liz And you haven't double-booked it for the evening?
Tony Course we haven't double-booked—this is a respectable hotel.
Liz Then whose is the overnight bag in the bathroom?
Tony Overnight bag?
Dick And whose is the handbag over there?
Tony Handbag? (*After a pause*) Listen—you like this gentleman, yes?
Liz Yes, he's very nice.
Tony (*to Dick*) And you like the lady?
Dick Yes, I do.
Tony Then that's all you need worry about. You got each other—you got champagne—you got dinner—you gotta bed. Stop asking questions where nobody's got the answers and get on enjoy yourselves!
Liz Sounds quite a good philosophy.
Tony Sure it's a good philosophy. I see a lotta life here, and that's the best philosophy of all—take it from me, signorina.
Liz Right. And it's signora by the way. I'm married.
Tony (*his eyes glazed*) Your husband coming too?
Liz No, he's in Manchester.
Tony That's good. Maybe he's got the second lady with him. (*He laughs*)
Liz If he has, good luck to him. (*She takes the menu*) Now, what's for dinner?
Tony (*beaming*) Now you talk my language. Dinner I can handle. What you like, sir?
Dick Anything as long as it's not pasta.

They study the menus

    Bob enters the R *room with a new packet of cigarettes*

Bob (*calling towards the bathroom*) All right in there?

    Kate comes out of the bathroom

Kate Yes. Except I left my bag next door with my lipstick in it. I won't be a second. (*She crosses towards the connecting door*)
Bob Right. (*Suddenly remembering*) No, don't . . .

Too late. Kate has opened the door and she enters the next room. She stops and everyone stares at each other. Bob flattens himself against the wall of the R *room*

Kate Oh, I'm terribly sorry. I—I thought this room was empty.

Dick No.
Tony No.
Kate No. (*At a loss*) Er . . .
Tony (*leaping into action*) It's all right, signorina—the gentleman he tell me to give it to these other people. He say you don't need it—you got a bed in there anyway—I mean a bath—I mean . . . I don't know what the hell I mean—but, er . . .
Kate Oh that's quite all right. It's just that I left my bag here.

Kate points to the bag where she left it earlier, beside the phone. Tony leaps to get it

Tony Don't move! I get it.
Kate (*to the other two*) I'm so sorry.
Dick It's all right.
Kate (*calling over her shoulder*) Dick?
Dick Yes?
Kate (*turning; puzzled*) Er—are you Dick?
Dick Yes.
Kate What a coincidence. I meant that Dick.
Dick Ah.
Kate (*calling*) Dick?
Bob (*grunting ambiguously from behind the wall*) Mm?
Kate You didn't tell me this room was taken.

Bob makes vague non-committal noises in his throat. Kate sees the champagne, and raises her eyebrows

    Champagne.
Dick Yes.
Kate How nice. Celebrating?
Dick Yes.
Kate What?
Liz My husband's birthday.

Bob freezes on hearing Liz's voice

Bob My God! My wife! (*He peers round the door-post, sees her back, and recoils, stunned*)
Dick (*getting a glass from the side*) Have a glass.
Kate Oh I couldn't . . .
Dick (*pouring*) Why not? It's on the house, isn't that so, Tony?

Tony nods his head dumbly

    And what about your friend next door?

Bob shakes his head equally dumbly

Kate (*calling as she takes the glass*) You've been offered a glass of champagne, Dick.
Bob (*replying hoarsely after several attempts*) No, thanks. I'm on Scotch.
Kate (*raising her glass*) Oh well—happy birthday, Dick.
Dick Er? Oh yes—thank you.

Act I

Tony (*frowning*) It's your birthday too?
Dick Seems like it. Do we get another bottle on the house?
Tony I don't know if Mr Tippett can afford it.
Liz (*evilly*) Oh, he can afford it. Bring another one. And one for them as well.
Kate Oh we couldn't.
Liz Yes, you could. Mr Tippett would love you to have a bottle. Put it all on the bill, Tony.
Kate Well—how very nice.
Tony Mama mia—this getting out of hand!
Kate Who is this Mr Tippett?
Liz He's an old, old friend of mine.
Tony You mean customer—that's different.
Liz (*her eyes narrowing*) I mean friend.
Tony Well he won't stay one for much longer at *this* rate! (*He gives Kate her bag*) Here your bag, signorina. I come and take your order for dinner in a minute. (*He mutters fiercely*) And that's *not* on Mr Tippett!
Kate (*taken aback*) Thank you. (*To the others*) It was nice meeting you.
Dick Join us for coffee later.
Kate Perhaps we will. Thank you.

Bob staggers, ashen-faced, away from the wall

Liz (*following Kate to the connecting door*) Just a moment.

Bob dives for cover under the table

Kate Yes?
Liz You wouldn't by any chance be called Mimi?
Kate No.
Liz I thought not. You don't look like a Mimi.
Tony (*to Liz*) *You're* called Mimi.
Liz Do *I* look like a Mimi?
Tony No.
Liz Right.
Tony (*scratching his head*) Two Dicks and no Mimis—I going crazy!

Liz returns to her place at the table as Kate goes through to the R room. She closes the connecting door and looks round for Bob

Kate (*heading for the bathroom*) Dick?

Bob emits a strangled moan, and emerges from beneath the table

   What are you doing there?

He makes gurgling noises

   Are you all right?

He nods dumbly

   Are you ill?

He shakes his head

Here—have a glass of champagne. That'll help.

She gives him a sip

It's from someone called Tippett.

He splutters into the glass. She hauls him to his feet

Look, sit down over here. You look terrible.

Bob Sorry. It's just—I just—had a bit of a shock.
Kate What kind of a shock? Not a heart attack?
Bob Er—possibly. A minor one. I get them sometimes.
Kate (*concerned*) My God! Shall I call a doctor? (*She goes to the phone*)
Bob No, no—please! It's not that serious.
Kate We should do something.
Bob It's all right, really.
Kate (*dialling*) But surely...
Bob I know! I've got some pills here. That's all I need. (*He fishes the small box of saccharin tablets from his pocket, and takes a pill. He grimaces at the taste*)
Kate (*peering over his shoulder*) Saccharin tablets?
Bob (*his face contorted*) No, no—I just keep them in that box.
Kate Well, as long as you're not going to die on me. I'd never get over that.
Bob Neither would I. (*The saccharin gets to him*) Yergh! (*He dashes towards the bathroom*)
Kate What is it?
Bob I'm allergic to them.

Bob exits

Kate (*musing*) Hypochondria as well as schizophrenia? (*She picks up the menu from the table and reads it*)

Next door, Liz and Dick have been studying their menus

Liz I'll have melon, followed by shish kebab, please.
Dick That sounds nice—so will I.
Tony (*writing down the orders*) OK. And another bottla champagne?
Liz Yes.
Tony (*taking back the menus*) I come back soon. Don't go away. Don't let any more people in the room. Don't give away any more bottlesa champagne. OK? I wanna keep my job a day or two longer.

Tony scurries out

Dick All go here, isn't it?
Liz Quite fun. I must do this more often.
Dick Do you suppose Geoffrey Tippett will keep paying the bills?
Liz No, unfortunately. You can't do it on a civil servant's earnings.
Dick You can on a psychiatrist's. I'll invite you again.
Liz That would be nice.
Dick There's just one thing I'm curious about. Will you excuse me a moment? (*He goes towards the main door*)

Act I

Liz Where are you going?
Dick I'll be back in a second.
Liz (*getting up*) What if Mimi turns up?
Dick Mark her "rejected goods" and send her back to Kew.

Dick goes

Tony enters the R room, where Kate has been studying the menu

Tony Now, signorina ... (*He looks around*) Where's the gentleman?
Kate Recovering from a heart attack in the bathroom.
Tony Heart attack?
Kate Well almost.
Tony I'm not surprised. Didn't he tell you that door was locked?
Kate It's not locked.
Tony It's supposed to be locked.
Kate How was I supposed to know that?
Tony Do you usually go wandering round hotels into strange bedrooms?
Kate (*indignantly*) That was part of our suite until ten minutes ago. How was I supposed to know we'd sublet it for birthday parties? On our champagne too!
Tony Mr Tippett's champagne.
Kate Who the hell *is* Mr Tippett anyway?
Tony Nona you business.
Kate (*angrily*) Look here—I'm getting a bit fed up with this!
Tony (*cooling down*) Sorry, sorry—I didn't mean that. I just get a bit hot under the shirt.
Kate Collar.
Tony Every place.

Bob comes out of the bathroom

Bob Ah, Tony!
Tony Si, signor?
Bob (*pointing next door*) How did that woman get there?
Tony What woman?
Bob That woman next door.
Tony (*out of the side of his mouth*) You know how she got here.
Bob No, I don't.
Tony (*fiercely*) Mr Tippett send her.
Bob Mr Tippett didn't send her.
Tony (*frantically*) Mr Tippett *did* send her!
Bob I tell you Mr Tippett *didn't* send her!
Tony Ah! Maybe that's why she's not called Mimi.
Bob (*thoughtfully*) On second thoughts I wonder if Mr Tippett *did* send her.
Tony (*angrily*) I wish the hell you make up your mind!
Kate What are you two talking about?
Bob Never mind.
Kate How do you know where she's from anyway?
Bob She, er—I er—she's one of my patients.
Kate Patients?

Bob Yes. I recognized her through the door.
Tony You a doctor?
Bob I'm a psychiatrist.
Tony I thought you worked with Mr Tippett?
Bob (*through gritted teeth*) I've never heard of Mr Tippett.
Tony (*befuddled*) Ah no that's right. He just pay for your champagne.
Bob Why has she followed me here—that's what I don't understand?
Kate It's just a coincidence.
Bob No, it's not.
Kate How do you know?
Bob Well, er—she's developed a crush on me, you see. One of those classic patient–doctor infatuations. She follows me everywhere. She'll ruin our whole evening.
Kate Does she always drag her husband along too?
Bob Her husband?
Kate The man with her.
Bob She said that?
Kate (*nodding*) They're celebrating his birthday. (*She raises her glass*) Hence the champagne.
Bob My God! (*He strides frantically about*) She's drinking champagne with another man!
Kate With her husband.
Bob (*impatiently*) Yes, yes, yes—that's beside the point!
Kate (*bemused*) Is it?
Bob (*to himself*) The point is, where does she think *I* am?
Kate What makes you so certain she knows you're here? Or cares?
Bob It's all too much of a coincidence. (*Frantically*) Oh my God—what am I going to do? What am I going to do?
Kate (*frowning*) It can't be *that* serious.
Bob It is! You don't understand—she's mad!
Kate How long have you known her?
Bob Twelve years.
Kate And she's still mad? You must be a rotten psychiatrist.
Bob I know! We'll go to a restaurant somewhere else.
Kate You hate restaurants.
Bob Do I?
Kate That's why you booked a private room in the first place. Claustrophobia as well as hypochondria and schizophrenia.
Bob (*ruffling his hair in despair*) How did I get into this situation? Why didn't I stay at home and spend a nice happy birthday in front of the television like everyone else does?
Kate Birthday?
Bob (*closing his eyes*) Oh no!
Kate Is it your birthday as well as her husband's?
Bob (*with a sigh*) Yes. Same names, same birthday. That's why she has a crush on me—confusion of identity. Excuse me—I need to consult myself. (*He sits in the armchair and buries his head in his hands*)

Act I   31

Tony (*shrugging at Kate*) I dunno why he's so worried. He's got two women and a Mimi still to come. Most men'd be very happy with that.
Kate I wish I understood it all.
Tony Don't try. *You* wanna end up one of his patients? Look, why don't you just order dinner while you're waiting?
Kate Right. I'll have pâté, followed by fillet steak. And bring the same for him.
Tony Well done?
Kate Better make it rare—we may not be here that long.
Tony That's the best news I've heard tonight.

Tony goes

Kate stares at Bob

Bob (*suddenly*) Ah!
Kate (*jumping*) Oh!
Bob I've got it! It's a plot. Geoff arranged for her to come!
Kate She knows Geoff too?
Bob (*caught*) Ah. Er—yes.
Kate Don't tell me *she* uses the agency?
Bob No, no—er—he's just a friend of hers.
Kate He gets around this Geoff. Who exactly is he?
Bob I've told you—Geoff Tippett, a friend.
Kate (*her eyes widening*) Tippett? *The* Tippett?
Bob Oh Lord!
Kate *The* Mister Tippett who provides champagne and dinner and women for all and sundry like there's no tomorrow! What is he—a one-man Welfare State?
Bob Now calm down, calm down—there's nothing to worry about.
Kate Who's worrying? We're obviously all just pawns in Geoff Tippett's hands. The only thing to do is lie back and enjoy it. (*Quickly*) I didn't mean that literally!
Bob (*scarcely listening*) We'll be all right as long as she doesn't find out we've been in there. (*A thought strikes him*) My God!
Kate Now what?
Bob My overnight bag. It's in their bathroom.
Kate So?
Bob She'll recognize it.
Kate *She* will recognize *your* overnight bag?
Bob Well, er—er—it's got my name on the tag.
Kate What are you doing with an overnight bag anyway? This is supposed to be just dinner, remember?
Bob Er—well I carry a lot of pills around. My hypochondria.
Kate (*cynically*) Really. Well if she's followed you here, she knows it's you, so it hardly matters anyway, does it?
Bob She may only suspect. But that would be proof. (*He paces up and down distractedly*) I must get that bag. I must get it back!

Kate Look, I'm feeling a bit spare here. Would you like me to leave you to work out your obsession with your patients and your pills and your overnight bags on your own?
Bob No, no—please don't go! I want more than anything to spend the evening with you.
Kate Well...
Bob It's just thrown me a bit seeing her. If you knew her you'd know why.
Kate I'd like to—she sounds fascinating. What's her name?
Bob (*fumbling*) Liz ... er—Mimi ... er ...
Kate It can't be Mimi.
Bob Why not?
Kate She asked me if *I* was Mimi.
Bob My God, she knows about Mimi!
Kate Who the hell *is* Mimi?
Bob Er—another friend of Geoff's.
Kate Silly of me to ask really.
Bob (*to himself*) But if she knows about Mimi, where does she suppose Mimi is?
Kate Probably organizing a coach party of all Geoff's other friends.
Bob I must get that bag!
Kate Well don't look at me.
Bob (*snapping his fingers*) Tony! Tony can get it. (*He dashes to the main door, and looks out*) He's gone. (*He thinks frantically*) Look—I'm just nipping out for a moment. I'll be back soon. Have some more champagne and wait for me.
Kate It hasn't arrived. Geoff probably hasn't paid for all the others yet.
Bob I'll get some. I'll get my bag. I'll get some dinner. I'll get everything. Just don't go away. I'll sort it all out I promise and then we'll celebrate my birthday in real style.
Kate You never told me it was your birthday.
Bob I'd forgotten.
Kate Amnesia too. I'm beginning to see why you're so lonely.

Bob hurries out into the corridor, closing the door

Kate opens her bag and touches up her lipstick

Dick enters the L room urgently

Liz What's the matter?
Dick I'm not supposed to be here.
Liz Wher are you supposed to be?
Dick (*pointing next door*) There.
Liz What do you mean?
Dick I've just checked the register. I was right in the first place—I'm booked into that room.
Liz Strange. And Geoff and I were booked into this one. You don't suppose...?
Dick Well then it would be Geoff and Mimi next door.
Liz Instead of Dick and somebody else.
Dick Exactly.

Act I

Liz It's just like musical chairs.
Dick Or beds.
Liz Don't jump the gun.
Dick Sorry, I didn't mean ...
Liz Let's stick to dinner-tables for the moment.
Dick Right.

> *Tony enters, pushing a dinner trolley covered with a large tablecloth. Unknown to Tony, Bob is concealed on the lower part of the trolley by the tablecloth. Tony wheels the trolley to the table*

Liz Well at least his timing's good.
Tony Now—signor, signorina—you like to take your seats please? (*He starts to set out the plates etc. with great aplomb*)

> *As Dick and Liz seat themselves the trolley moves of its own accord towards the bathroom. Bob appears from beneath the trolley and scuttles on his haunches to the bathroom. Tony does a double-take on finding the trolley has changed places*

> *Bob slips into the bathroom and closes the door*

> *The others turn at the sound of the door closing*

Liz What was that?
Tony The draught from the other door, signorina.
Liz You opened that seconds ago.
Tony Draughts travel very slowly in this hotel. (*He holds out the bottle of champagne for Dick to view*) Your champagne, sir.
Dick Splendid, splendid.

> *Tony places it in the ice-bucket and turns to the melon*

Tony Melon for the signorina.
Liz Thank you.

> *Tony serves the melon, scattering bits of fruit with huge élan*

Tony How's that?
Dick I'm glad we didn't order soup.
Tony I bring your shish kebab soon. Buon appetito!

> *Bob crawls out of the bathroom to see the trolley disappearing out of reach, forcing him to retreat back to the bathroom. Tony wheels the trolley out to the corridor, closing the door behind him*

Liz (*picking up her spoon*) Buon appetito.
Dick (*preoccupied*) Yes. Definitely.
Liz (*holding out the ginger bowl*) Ginger?
Dick Thank you. (*He takes it, still preoccupied, puts two large spoonfuls into his champagne and stirs the glass*)
Liz Sugar's there.
Dick Thank you. (*He picks up the salt and scatters it liberally over his melon*)
Liz Are you all right?
Dick Mm?

Liz What are you worried about?
Dick Worried? Who's worried? I'm not worried. (*He takes a bite of melon, freezes, goes red, and finally chokes. He takes a swig of champagne and spits it out over the carpet*)

Dick clutches his throat, staggers to his feet, and hurries into the bathroom

A short pause while Liz stares in bemusement

Dick comes out of the bathroom again, white-faced. He closes the door, moves in a trance and sits at the table

Liz What's the matter now?
Dick (*in a hoarse voice*) There's a man in the bathroom.
Liz A man?
Dick Yes.
Liz What's he doing?
Dick Trying to climb out of the window.
Liz We're five floors up!
Dick Perhaps he's trying to commit suicide.
Liz You're sure you're not having hallucinations now?

He shakes his head. She rises slowly, and goes very cautiously towards the bathroom. She is just about to put her hand on the door handle, when the door opens

A strange figure appears. It is Bob—a very bristly beard round his jaw, a turban made from a white towel round his head, and sunglasses on his nose. He carries his overnight bag under one arm, and the handle of a toilet-brush in the other hand

Bob (*in a heavy Indian accent*) Oh excuse me, please—excuse me. I am most sorry to interrupt. I am just inspecting the rooms to see that everything is sanitary. Please to continue your most delectable meal. My felicitations to all and sundry. Good-night.

Bob goes out to the corridor, closing the door

The others sit frozen, staring at the door

Bob bursts into the R room

Kate screams. He comes towards her

It's all right. It's only me.
Kate Keep away from me! Keep away! Don't touch me!

Kate rushes screaming into the bathroom, slamming the door. Tony enters the R room from the corridor pushing the trolley, then stops, staring

Bob (*going after her*) No, no, please!

As he hammers on the door, Tony smashes him over the head with the champagne bottle (false bottle—padded turban), and Bob collapses on the floor

CURTAIN

ACT II

The same. A few moments later

When the CURTAIN *rises Bob sits, in the* R *room, splayed out in the armchair, holding his "beard" in his hand, while Kate fans him with his "turban". Tony looks on. In the* L *room, a bemused Liz and Dick are at the table*

Dick He nearly gave me a heart attack.
Kate You nearly gave me a heart attack.
Liz He nearly gave *me* a heart attack!
Tony He nearly gave *me* a heart attack!
Bob I nearly gave myself a heart attack!
Tony I go see if they've had a heart attack next door.

Tony goes out to the corridor, taking the empty trolley with him

Kate We'd better all take one of your heart pills.
Bob Just keep doing that. It's nice.

Kate continues fanning him

Tony enters the L *room*

Tony Everything OK, signor?
Dick Tony, do sanitary inspectors usually come round during dinner?
Tony Si, signor. Most of the guests are in the restaurant then, you see.
Liz How did he get in there in the first place?
Tony Er—he come up a ladder and climb in the window.
Dick Wouldn't it be simpler to just knock on the door, and walk through?
Tony We don't allow him in the bedrooms.
Dick Why not?
Tony Er—he is an untouchable. Now, I go and get your next course, yes?
Dick If you're quite sure it's safe to leave us. There won't be any CND marches or SAS raiding parties coming through here, will there?
Tony No more interruptions, I promise. (*To himself*) Please God!

Tony goes out

Liz and Dick continue eating

Kate (*stopping her fanning*) There! Have your turban back.
Bob (*taking the towel*) Thank you.
Kate How's your head?
Bob Just saved from splintering by this.
Kate (*trying on his "beard"*) What was your beard made from?
Bob The end of a lavatory brush.

Kate (*dropping it hastily*) How insanitary.
Bob I don't think so. It hasn't been used for years. I need a drink. (*He sees the champagne*) Is that champagne?
Kate Yes. That's what Tony hit you with.
Bob Well at least he didn't break the bottle. Where did it come from?
Kate Geoff Tippett, naturally.
Bob (*muttering*) God—I hope he can afford all this.

Bob and Kate sit at the table, and he starts to uncork the champagne

Dick (*putting down his fork*) This is an absurd situation! I'm supposed to be dining with a Mimi, who's taken the place of a Kate, and here I am with a Liz—none of whom I've ever met before!
Liz Isn't it fun?
Dick Oh, it's very nice—please don't misunderstand me. It's just that ... well, where *is* Mimi? She might still turn up.
Liz She might.
Dick And where is Geoff Tippett. *He* might turn up.
Liz He might.
Dick Worst of all, they might turn up together.
Liz Then we'll just have to order some more champagne. Stop worrying and enjoy your melon. More ginger?
Dick (*hastily*) No thank you!

Dick goes back to his melon. Meanwhile Bob is absent-mindedly polishing his knife on his tie

Kate (*watching; intrigued*) Is that to clean the knife, or trim the tie?
Bob Sorry, it's a habit of mine—when I'm worried.
Kate What are you worried about now?
Bob I can't understand what she's doing next door.
Kate For heaven's sake! Couldn't it wait? The evening's going by, and so far you've paid more attention to her than to me.
Bob I'm sorry. My professional preoccupation. (*He raises his champagne glass*) Here's to us.
Kate That's better.

They are about to drink, when he stops again

Bob There's another thing.
Kate Now what?
Bob How much does she know about Mimi?
Kate (*getting angry*) What does it matter what she knows about Mimi? Who cares what anybody knows about Mimi? Who the hell *is* Mimi anyway?
Bob Well she keeps coming up in the conversation, so she's obviously expected.
Kate (*close to tears*) Can we please have dinner and talk about ourselves for a bit, and forget about all your friends and patients and *their* friends and husbands, and anyone else of the several hundred people who might be visiting this hotel tonight?
Bob You are overwrought, aren't you? Are you feeling all right?

Act II

Kate (*exasperated*) Ohhhh!
Bob Sorry, sorry—I didn't mean that.
Kate What's the *matter* with you?
Bob I'm just nervous when there are loose ends around the place. It's my civil service training.
Kate Civil service? What's that got to do with psychiatry?
Bob (*floundering*) Ah ... well, I—I'm sometimes civil to the second service ... er—seconded to serve the civil psych—— I'm a second psych ...
Kate You're employed by the government?
Bob Why couldn't I put it like that?
Kate Perhaps it's working for the government that makes you so neurotic.
Bob (*frantically scraping butter on to his toast with his knife*) Neurotic? Who's neurotic?
Kate You are. I've never met anyone so neurotic in my life! What are you trying to do now—make fire?
Bob (*ceasing his scraping*) Sorry. Let's eat.
Kate That's the most un-neurotic thing you've said all evening.

They start to eat. There is a moment's silence between the rooms as all four enjoy dinner

Bob
Dick (*together*) Mmm—delicious!
Kate
Liz (*together*) Yes, isn't it?

Pause

Bob
Dick (*together*) More champagne?
Kate
Liz (*together*) Thank you.

The two men pour simultaneously

Bob
Dick (*together*) Cheers.
Kate
Liz (*together*) Cheers.

All four clink glasses and drink. All commence eating again

Tony enters the L room, pushing the trolley

Tony You ready for your kebab?
Dick Just about. You can serve it up.
Tony Everything OK now?
Dick Everything's fine, thank you.
Tony That's good. I like everyone to be happy.
Liz Is everyone happy next door?
Tony Next door?
Liz That nice man who says he's called Dick and that nice girl who isn't called Mimi, whose suite we seem to be sharing.

Tony I think so. I go find out in a minute. (*He starts to toss salad around like a juggler*)
Dick (*after watching for a moment*) Now I know why it's called tossed salad.

An onion flies into the air, and Tony deftly catches it

Liz With spring onions.
Tony (*putting the dishes on the table*) Presto!
Liz Thank you.
Tony (*wheeling away the trolley*) Now I go serve them next door.
Liz Oh, Tony.
Tony Si, signora?
Liz Be sure to tell them next door that on no account are we to be disturbed, will you? We want to be alone.

Quick pause. The two men stare at her

Tony (*meaningfully*) Si, signora! Certainly, signora! Er—does that mean you not having coffee?
Liz Not unless we call you.
Tony And if Mimi come—who's having her?
Liz You can—on the house.
Tony (*beaming*) OK. Prego! Buena serra, Mimi! Arrivederci! Buon appetito!

Tony goes, riding the trolley like a scooter through the door

Dick What was all that about?
Liz (*innocently*) What?
Dick All that about being alone?
Liz Well don't you want to be?
Dick Yes, but er—we did invite them for coffee earlier.
Liz I'd rather have coffee with just you.
Dick You've cancelled coffee.
Liz Then I'd rather *not* have coffee with just you.
Dick Ah. Splendid, splendid.
Liz Wouldn't you like me to be your soulmate unlimited for just one evening? (*She goes and listens surreptitiously at the connecting door*)
Dick (*nervously fiddling with his kebab*) Yes, yes, indeed, indeed.

She comes behind him and strokes his head. He drops the kebab

Liz (*taking hold of his hands*) What *is* the matter with you? Your hands are shaking.
Dick I've never been in this situation before. You're married and your husband might ...
Liz My husband is busy elsewhere at the moment, so let's forget about him. (*She strokes his brow*)
Dick Oh Lord!
Liz What's wrong?
Dick It's just that—well I'm allergic to married women.
Liz Allergic!

Act II   39

Dick Yes—you see it's always the married ones who seem to become infatuated with their therapists. It's caused me such trouble over the years that I've developed this—phobia you see.

Liz Well, as a psychiatrist wouldn't you say the best way to tackle a phobia is to meet it head on?

Dick What do you mean?

Liz (*holding him*) Allay your fears by proving them wrong.

Dick (*backing away*) Well, I—I'm not so sure, I——

Liz (*following him*) Present yourself with a challenge, and conquer it.

Dick I don't think I could. I——

Liz Goodness—you're shaking all over. You'd better lie down for a moment. Here, let me help you.

She guides him towards the bed

Dick Where are we going?

Tony enters the R room with the trolley

Tony Here we are. Two fillet steak.

Liz lets down the bed

Dick Oh, no, no.

It hits the floor with a thud. Next door, the others look up

Bob What was that?

Tony Mama mia! They don't waste a lotta time.

Bob What was it?

Tony The bed.

Bob The bed!

Liz guides Dick on to the bed

Liz Now just lie down and relax.

Dick Oh God, help me please!

She sits by him and strokes his head. Next door, Bob is staring at the connecting door

Bob What do they want the bed for?

Tony What do people usually want a bed for? I tell you, they crazy about each other.

Bob How do you know?

Tony I see a lotta life here, sir. I know when two people got the hots for each other.

Bob (*staring back at the door*) The hots?

Tony Oh—and they told me to tell you, on no account they to be disturbed.

Bob (*rising*) Good God! (*He paces up and down in an agony of indecision*) I can't stand it, I can't stand it! What's he doing to her?

Tony You wanna demonstration?

Bob It's no good—I can't go through with this. It's gone far enough. Forgive me, Kate.

Kate What for?
Bob I should never have tried it in the first place. I must put a stop to it here and now.
Kate (*bewildered*) What . . .?

He strides to the connecting door, throws it open and enters the L *room, where Liz and Dick are reclining on the bed. During the following, Tony follows Bob and hovers in the connecting doorway*

Bob Right—*pax, pax*! All over. Let's call it a day.
Dick (*sitting up*) What?
Bob I give in. Surrender. It's all my fault. Let's call a truce.
Dick (*to Liz*) What's he talking about?
Liz I haven't the faintest idea.
Dick (*to Bob*) Are you Geoff Tippett?
Bob (*furiously*) No, I am *not* Geoff Tippett!
Dick Then who are you?
Bob (*indicating Liz*) She knows. I don't know what you're up to, but let's call it quits, can we, darling?
Dick "Darling"?
Bob Yes, "darling"!
Dick Is this who I think it is?
Bob I'm her husband.
Dick (*nodding*) That's who I thought it was.
Liz (*frowning*) Husband?
Bob I don't know what she's told you, old man, but I apologize for everything.
Liz What do you mean, husband?
Bob What do you mean, what do I mean?
Dick Isn't he your husband?
Liz My husband's in Manchester.
Bob I'm not, I'm here.
Dick Then who's this?
Liz I've never seen him before in my life.
Bob Oh for God's sake! Let's not play games now, sweetheart.
Liz (*indignantly*) Don't you "sweetheart" me!
Bob Look the game's over. The pretence is finished. It's all gone wrong. I'm sorry about it.
Liz (*to Dick*) I don't know what he's talking about.
Dick You really mean it? This isn't your husband?
Bob Of course I'm her husband!
Liz Not remotely like my husband.
Dick Then who is he?
Liz I haven't the faintest idea. He must be playing games.
Bob Playing games? *You're* the one who's playing games!
Liz Oh do stop it, and go away.
Bob (*beside himself*) I will *not* go away! (*To Dick*) Look, my friend——
Dick I'm no friend of yours!

Act II   41

Bob I know, but you're being hoodwinked. This is my wife, Liz—and I'm her husband, Bob——
Liz No you're not—you're Dick.
Bob Dick?
Dick That's right. Your girl friend said so.
Bob (*to Liz*) You know bloody well I'm not Dick!
Dick Then why did she call you Dick?
Bob Because she thinks I'm you.
Dick (*puzzled*) She thinks you're me?
Bob Yes. You see, she'd never met me before...
Dick She's never met *me* before.
Bob Which is why I was able to pretend I was you.
Dick *You've* never met me before.
Bob No, but you see...
Dick (*to Tony, who is hovering in the doorway*) Had *you* ever met him before?
Tony No, signor.
Bob Thanks a lot!
Liz And he's never met *me* before.
Bob (*furiously*) Oh shut up!
Dick How dare you speak to my guest like that?
Bob She's not your guest—she's my wife!
Dick It seems to me she ought to know whose wife she is, and she says she's never met you before. What's more, no-one in this room has ever met you before. If I were you, I'd go away before I got into trouble.
Bob (*desperately*) Liz, please! I'm sorry about it all. Let's go somewhere and talk it over.
Liz How do you know my name is Liz?
Bob Oh for Christ's sake!
Liz (*to Tony*) Did you tell him my name was Liz?
Tony (*shaking his head*) I thought your name was Mimi.
Bob (*to Dick, apoplectic*) I've always known her name was Liz! I *married* her when her name was Liz!
Liz How could you? You're not my husband.
Bob (*tearing his hair*) Ahhhh!
Dick (*to Tony*) This fellow looks as if he's a bit mad. Do you think you could get rid of him for us?
Tony (*wavering*) I don't know, sir, I——
Bob (*crouching like a wild animal*) Don't you touch me! Don't anyone come near me!
Dick (*going to Bob*) Come on, my friend——
Bob I'm no friend of yours!
Dick No, you're not—so would you please leave us alone to enjoy our dinner in peace?
Bob Dinner? You were enjoying a lot more than dinner by the looks of it. If you think I'm going to leave you and my wife to——
Dick She's not your wife, and you're not staying here. Tony, will you give me a hand to get this gentleman to leave.

Bob Don't you lay a hand on me!
Dick Come on now, old chap...

Bob leaps on to the bed and starts hurling pillows and bed clothes around. During the following, Kate comes and stands in the connecting doorway, watching. Dick and Tony close on Bob. There is a highly undignified brawl, during which Tony gets someone's elbow in his eye, Dick gets kicked in the stomach, and Bob gets his head stuck in the ice-bucket. Kate—in the doorway—and Liz watch from opposite sidelines. Eventually Dick seizes the opportunity to grab the bedspread and throw it over Bob's head

   Grab him, Tony!

Tony recovers to grasp the shrouded Bob in a bear-hug. Dick picks up the champagne bottle, and lifts it to crown Bob with it

Kate
Liz } (*together*) No!!

He stops

Bob (*muffled*) All right, all right—I give in! I give in!
Dick You'll leave?
Bob Yes.
Dick You'll go quietly?
Bob Yes.
Dick You promise?
Bob *Yes!*
Dick Very well.

He nods to Tony, who cautiously removes the bedspread. Dick stands with bottle at the ready, as Bob emerges, looking distinctly dishevelled. He sees the bottle, and makes a placatory gesture

Bob Not again, please—I'm not a ship. I'm going. (*He goes to the connecting door, and turns, pointing at Liz*) Don't think you've won though. There are other ways.

He goes through to the next room, Kate backing before him, and closes the door. She stares at him, terrified, and shies away as he approaches

   Don't worry, I'm not going to attack you.
Kate Where are you going?
Bob To look in the mirror and see if I'm me.

   Bob goes into the bathroom

Next door, the others breathe sighs of relief

Dick What an extraordinary fellow!
Liz Quite mad.
Tony (*nursing his eye*) I knew he crazy from the start.
Dick Who is he, Tony?
Tony Some friend of Mr Tippett's.

Act II

Dick That name again.
Liz I can't think what the connection is. Unless he's taken Geoff's place in order to get a free evening at his expense.
Dick Most peculiar.
Liz (*to Dick*) How are you feeling?
Dick (*collapsing in the armchair*) A bit weak. It's all too much excitement for a simple psychiatrist like me.
Liz Here, put some ice on your forehead.

Liz collects some ice from the ice-bucket into the napkin, and holds it to his head

Tony You want some coffee now, after all?
Liz I think perhaps we'd better.
Tony Me too. I get some.
Liz How's your eye?
Tony It's OK. I got another one.

Tony goes. Next door, Bob comes out of the bathroom again, looking more respectable

Bob Right—I've decided what to do.
Kate (*nervously*) Oh dear.
Bob Don't worry—it's quite safe. It's what I should have done at the start.
Kate What's that?
Bob I'm going to tell you what's happened.
Kate Another story?
Bob No, the truth. Sit down.
Kate I'm not sure that——
Bob (*gently*) Please, sit down. I'm quite harmless really, I promise. (*He pours her some champagne*) Here. (*He gives her the glass, and sits opposite her*) Now this is the situation. Are you listening?
Kate Yes.
Bob I'm not Dick. I'm Bob.
Kate Bob.
Bob Yes. That's your Dick through there—the one you came to meet.
Kate Dick.
Bob Only you met me by accident, because I was here to meet Mimi...
Kate Mimi.
Bob Who was supposed to be a birthday present to me from Geoff...
Kate Geoff.
Bob But when you turned up instead, I thought you were Mimi.
Kate Mimi.
Bob And I liked you so much, that when I found out you weren't, I pretended to be Dick.
Kate Dick.
Bob Who is actually through there with the woman who, though she denies it, is my wife Liz.
Kate Liz.
Bob She has obviously formed a conspiracy of some sort with Geoff——

Kate Geoff.
Bob —who cooked up the story about Mimi——
Kate Mimi.
Bob —in order to get me back together with Liz——
Kate Liz.
Bob —but instead of finding me in there she found Dick——
Kate Dick.
Bob —because I'd arranged that he be taken there by Tony——
Kate Tony.
Bob —in order to pass him off on Mimi——
Kate Mimi.
Bob —because I wanted to be here with you.
Kate Me.
Bob You're Kate.
Kate Kate.
Bob That's right. Do you understand?

Long pause

Kate No.
Bob But it's so simple! There's only one fact you really need to know. The Dick you arranged to meet through "Soulmates Unlimited"—Dick the psychiatrist—is that man through there. Now he doesn't realize that you're here. I suggest you go and tell him.

Pause

Kate And then what?
Bob Then he'll have to choose between you and my wife.
Kate I see.
Bob I'm sorry. It was a piece of gross deception on my part, and ridiculous of me to think I could get away with it, but I—well I just thought you were rather nice, you see . . . and as I'm not a Mimi sort of chap anyway . . . and as my marriage is rather on the rocks . . . well I thought I'd just take the chance that seemed to be offered.
Kate Ah.
Bob Silly of me. I should have known better.

Pause

Well, hadn't you better go and introduce yourself?
Kate Right. (*She walks as if in a dream towards the connecting door. There she turns*) What are you going to do?
Bob Sit here and polish the cutlery.

She looks at him for a second, then turns and goes through the connecting door. Liz and Dick look up as she enters

Kate I'm Kate.

Pause

Dick Kate?

Act II

Kate Yes.
Dick *The* Kate?
Kate Yes.
Dick The Kate who works in a boutique, and likes cats and antiques and country walks?
Kate Yes.
Dick Good Lord! I thought you weren't coming.
Kate I did.
Dick But——
Kate It's all a bit of a mix-up which I don't quite understand myself, but the main fact is that I'm here, and I'm supposed to be having dinner with you.
Dick I see.

Pause. He looks from Kate to Liz, and back

Well what do we do now?
Liz What do you want to do now?
Dick I—I—don't know.
Liz Well, as I seem to be the intruder, I'd better go away and leave you two to begin what should have been begun at the beginning.
Dick Oh no, don't—please ...
Liz What else do you suggest?
Dick (*wavering*) I don't know. I er—that is, I er—what I mean is, I er ...
Liz What you mean is, you want someone to make the decision for you. Well, I'm making it. (*She gets her handbag and heads for the main door*)
Dick Where are you going?
Liz To the restaurant, to have my coffee—and possibly a couple of brandies with it. As I've lost both my husband and my substitute partner for the evening, I may as well get sloshed on my own in style. Arrivederci!

Liz goes

Dick and Kate stare at each other awkwardly

Dick What an astonishing evening.
Kate Yes. (*She giggles*)
Dick Well, er—champagne?
Kate (*hiccuping*) No thank you. I think I've had enough. (*She giggles*)

Pause

Dick So ... you're Kate.
Kate Yes.
Dick Extraordinary.
Kate Yes.

Pause

Dick How are your cats?
Kate Fine.
Dick Good.

Pause

Kate How's the psychiatry business?
Dick Booming.
Kate Good. (*After a quick pause*) Or bad.

Long pause. She stifles a giggle

Dick } (*together*) { Would you like to——?
Kate }   { How did you come to——?
Dick } (*together*) Sorry.
Kate }

Pause

The door opens, and Tony enters with a tray of coffee. He now sports a dashing eye-patch

Tony Presto—coffee!
Dick Ah, thank you. Is that eye all right?
Tony (*putting down the tray*) Sure. I tell everyone I got it dealing with a gang of terrorists. (*He notices Kate*) Hey—what the hell you doing here?
Kate I've joined him for coffee.
Tony Where the other signora?
Dick Gone to the restaurant for coffee.
Tony Where the other signor?
Kate Next door.
Tony By himself?
Dick Unless Mimi's arrived.
Tony Mama mia! You people certainly get around. I see a lotta life here—I never seen life like the lot I seen here tonight. Well—you got all you need? Coffee there—sugar there—cream there—and bed there. I take it you don't wanna be disturbed like you didn't wanna be disturbed the last time?
Dick Yes—thank you.
Tony OK. (*At the door*) Any more fights, don't ask for me—just call in United Nations.

Tony goes

Awkward pause

Dick Would you like coffee?
Kate No, thank you.
Dick Would you like to sit down?
Kate No, thank you.
Dick Would you like to kiss me?
Kate No, thank you.

Pause

Dick Would you like to go back next door?
Kate Yes, please.
Dick I thought so.
Kate Would you like me to get her back from the restaurant?

Act II

Dick Yes, I would, but . . .
Kate What?
Dick It's not as easy as that, is it?
Kate No.
Dick Do you suppose that really *is* her husband?
Kate Yes.
Dick Yes, I thought so. She was just angry with him, wasn't she?
Kate Yes.
Dick Can't blame her really.
Kate No.
Dick So what do we do?
Kate I don't know.

Pause

Dick Do you really like him?
Kate Yes. I don't know why. He's impossible. (*After a pause*) Do you like her?
Dick Yes. Though I haven't much hope. *I'm* impossible.
Kate Do they like each other?
Dick Not much, I gather. Though you never know with married people.
Kate Don't you?
Dick No. I know. I've been one myself.
Kate I haven't.
Dick Lucky you.
Kate I wish I had.
Dick There you are, you see. The eternal dilemma. Those who aren't married want to be married—those who are married don't want to be married. Those who aren't married who *don't* want to be married are perverts—those who are married who want to *stay* married are freaks. Daft system.
Kate It still doesn't help us to know what to do.
Dick I suppose the only way to find that out is to find out what *they* want to do.
Kate Yes.
Dick Which we can't do while she's down there and he's up here—not speaking to each other.
Kate No.
Dick We need to get them together, in order to break them apart—if you see what I mean.
Kate How do we do that?

He thinks

Dick I know. I'll send her a message that I want to see her back here again. You go and tell him that there's a Mimi just arrived, who he must deal with. Then we'll leave them to it.
Kate He'll run a mile.
Dick Be firm. Tell him it's his responsibility to get rid of her. If he won't face that one, then he's not worth knowing anyway.

Kate Would you face it?
Dick No—but then I'm not worth knowing anyway.
Kate (*smiling*) You're sweet.
Dick Careful. You'll fall for me next, and that would complicate things still further.
Kate No, I won't. (*She turns towards the connecting door*)
Dick Just a sec. Wait till I've phoned. (*He goes to the phone and dials*) Room service? Is Tony there please? ... Tony—would you mind going to the restaurant and telling that lady that I'd like to see her back here again please? ... Yes, Tony, I—— No, Tony, I—— Quite, Tony, I—— (*Suddenly he lets fly a stream of invective in fluent Italian. Then smiling sweetly*) Thank you, Tony. (*He replaces the receiver*) Wonderful what a bit of politeness can do.

Dick picks up his umbrella, gestures to Kate, and goes out to the corridor

Kate goes through to the next room

Kate (*to Bob*) Hello. I'm back.
Bob What happened?
Kate It's got a bit more complicated.
Bob Impossible.
Kate Someone called Mimi's on her way up.
Bob Impossible.
Kate We think you ought to deal with her.
Bob *Totally* impossible. I thought Mimi didn't exist.
Kate Apparently she does.
Bob What can I do with her?
Kate Whatever one does with a Mimi. (*She pours herself more champagne*)
Bob I don't think I'm capable.
Kate Well you must do something. She's arriving next door any minute. (*She hiccups and raises her glass to him*)
Bob Haven't you had enough of that?
Kate No. (*She drinks*)
Bob Where are the others?
Kate They've er—made themselves scarce.
Bob Why don't we all make ourselves scarce?
Kate You can't just leave her to sit about in an empty room on her own.
Bob Be quite a nice rest for her, I should imagine.
Kate (*taking his arm, and propelling him towards the connecting door*) Go on. Send her away—if that's what you want.
Bob It is.
Kate Then do it.

He starts, and stops again

Bob *You* won't go away, will you?
Kate No.

He repeats the movement

Bob Can I ask just one thing first?

Act II

Kate What?
Bob Will you kiss me?

Quick pause

Kate I don't kiss married men.
Bob Neither do I ... I mean I don't kiss married women ... I mean I don't ... I never kiss anybody.

She kisses him hesitantly

   Oh Lord!
Kate Go on.

In a trance, he goes through to the next room. There is a knock on the door of the R room. She goes to open the main door

   Dick sticks his head in

Dick Has he gone?
Kate Yes.
Dick Good. She should be up any minute.

He goes to the connecting door and listens, with Kate close behind him. He turns and holds out a hand

   Good luck.

Kate (*shaking hands*) And to you. (*She hiccups and giggles*)

They listen together at the door. Next door, there is a knock

Bob (*fearfully*) Come in.

   Tony enters the L room

Tony (*brusquely*) Now listen to me, signor—— (*Seeing Bob*) What you doing here?
Bob Er—waiting.
Tony What for?
Bob I daren't tell you.
Tony I can take it.
Bob A lady.
Tony Where the other signor?
Bob Gone.
Tony Where?
Bob With the other lady.
Tony (*totally losing his cool*) Whassa matter with you people? You crazy—all of you! You lost your screws! First you wanna be here with one chick—then you wanna be in there with another chick while the other guy in here with the first chick—then you wanna break him up with that chick and get him together with the other chick—then he send me to get the first chick back while you in there with the other chick—then he goes off with the other chick while you waiting here for the first chick! I don't know why the four of you don't go and live in a cement mixer together. You'd be very happy.

Bob It is a bit complicated—I'm sorry.
Tony Anyway, the other chick's on her way up from the restaurant.

Next door, Dick claps his hands to his head

Bob Which chick—er lady is that?
Tony Which one you think? The lady you were meant to see, who you didn't want to see, who the other guy was seeing, who you didn't want her to see. He sent me to see her.
Bob The lady who's not called Mimi?
Tony That's right.
Bob Yes, I thought so—it's a plot.
Tony You guys try any more plots, you gonna chase your tails up your own backsides!
Bob They want to leave us together, so *they* can go off together. I knew it was too good to last.

Next door, Dick and Kate exchange glances

(*Collapsing into the armchair*) I can't take all this. Bring us a couple of cognacs will you, Tony—I think we're going to need them.
Tony *You* need them? What about me?
Bob And one for yourself.
Tony On Mr Tippett's bill? Naturally—don't answer that. (*He goes towards connecting door*) I see if everything OK next door. Or is there a party going on there too?
Bob No, it's probably empty.
Tony You wanna look?
Bob No thank you. I'd rather not know.

Tony bends down, takes out the key of the connecting door and peers through the keyhole. Dick and Kate have flattened themselves against the wall. She hiccups and giggles. He puts his hand over her mouth

Tony I can't see nobody.
Bob That's what I thought.
Tony (*trying to put the key back in*) Hey, wait a minute. I see what's wrong with the lock. The key's too short. Maybe he work from the other side. (*He opens the door and tries the key*) See? He work fine now.
Bob Pity you didn't discover that earlier. It would have saved a lot of trouble. A stitch in time, and all that.
Tony Don't you gimme none of you crummy English proverbs! Pity you people have to open doors before the horse has bolted and let an ill-wind blow the shit in the fan! Anyway I gonna lock it now and try and keep you lot in one place for five minutes. (*He goes through to the next room, shuts the door and locks it*)

Dick and Kate grab him

Ahhh!
Dick Shhh. (*In a whisper*) Just keep quite, Tony, and don't ask any questions.

Act II 51

Tony Why should I ask any questions? I'd be too scared you might gimme some answers.
Dick We just want to wait here quietly and see what happens next door.
Tony Why not? The end of the world gotta come sometime. Me—I ain't gonna wait for it. I got work to do. I leaving you crazy people to cook in your own gravy.

Tony exits

Dick Talking of gravy—have you had dinner yet?
Kate We didn't get further than the first course.
Dick Neither did we. (*He investigates the trolley*) There are two luke-warm fillet steaks here. Shall we have them?
Kate Why not?

He sits Kate at the table, and starts to serve the steaks. Kate giggles

Are you sure this is a good idea?
Dick Why not?
Kate We might be arranging a reconciliation next door, not a bust-up.
Dick Never. He came here specifically for a dirty night out with Mimi, didn't he?
Kate (*frowning*) I think that was the idea.
Dick Well if that *is* his wife I'd like to see him talk his way out of that one!
Kate What did *she* come here for though?
Dick A very *un*dirty night out with Geoff Tippett. She told me.
Kate They might just end up having a dirty night out together.
Dick Impossible.
Kate Why?
Dick They're married.

Next door Bob is nervously polishing a knife with his tie. There is a knock. He jumps and cuts his tie in half, stares at the end in his hand, then stuffs it into his pocket

Bob (*muttering*) All right, Robert old man—get it over with. (*He goes and opens the main door*)

Mimi (Liz in disguise) stands there. She has an exotic hair-do, large sunglasses, and a tight dress

Mimi Hi. I'm Mimi.

Bob slams the door shut. He recovers and opens the door again

Bob I'm sorry. I wasn't expecting you.

Mimi enters

Mimi What you mean, darlin'? If you ain't expectin' me what you doin' here?
Bob Well, yes I was expecting you. But then I wasn't. Then again I was—but I wasn't.

Mimi (*nodding*) Makes sense. I'm sorry I'm late, sweetheart. Had a busy day.
Bob Doing what?

She just looks at him

Oh, sorry er . . .
Mimi You're sweet!
Bob Good Lord. You really do exist then?
Mimi Well if I don't darlin', a lot of people are not getting value for money. (*She sees the coffee*) Oh dear, am I too late for dinner?
Bob I'm afraid so.
Mimi Never mind. We've better things to do.
Bob Er, yes.
Mimi So you're Bob, eh?
Bob I think so, I'm not quite sure.
Mimi (*sitting in the armchair and patting the arm*) Well, Bob—come and tell me about yourself.
Bob I'd love to but I have a slight problem.
Mimi (*nodding*) Yes, Geoff told me. But I'm sure we can sort it out together, lover.
Bob No, you don't understand. It's my wife.
Mimi I understand.
Bob No, you don't understand. I'm afraid I can't manage it . . .
Mimi I understand.
Bob (*frantically*) No, you *don't* understand. She's—she's . . .

There is a knock at the main door

She's here. Oh my God! (*He rushes backwards and forwards between Mimi and the door*)
Mimi Your wife? Here?
Bob Yes! Please—you must go. (*He tries the connecting door. It is locked*) Oh Lord. You must hide! The bathroom!

He takes her arm and tries to guide her to the bathroom. She evades him and goes to the bed

Mimi Don't be silly, darlin'. I'm not skulking in the bathroom like a silly school-girl. (*She makes herself comfortable on the bed*) If it's your wife tell her you're busy and send her packin'.
Bob I can't do that! I can't just . . . Please, you must hide!
Mimi I've been given my orders, lover, and I'm stoppin' right here.
Bob Orders?

Another knock

Oh my God!

Bob lifts the bed, Mimi and all, up into the alcove

There is a squeal as Mimi disappears

Bob checks the room, sees her bag, flings it into the fridge then opens the door

Act II

Tony stands there with a tray and two cognacs

Tony (*Furiously*) Oh, it's you! Why have you started knocking all of a sudden?
Bob It's polite to knock.
Tony You never knocked before!
Bob Before I knew what was in the room. Now I don't know what the hell I might find! (*He comes into the room*) Here your cognacs.
Tony Oh, thank you. I forgot I'd ordered them.
Bob Where the lady?
Tony She's er—not here yet.

There is a muffled cry from the alcove. They both look at it. Tony looks back at Bob

That's another lady.

Pause

Tony (*glazed*) *Another* lady?
Bob Yes.
Tony Who? Don't answer that—I don't wanna know.

Bob lets down the bed with a dishevelled Mimi on board

Bob This is Mimi.
Mimi Hi.
Tony (*hoarsely*) Mama mia! (*He goes closer and stares*) You Mimi?
Mimi (*nodding*) Me Mimi.
Tony You're late. You missed all the fun.
Mimi Seemed to me it was just beginning.
Tony (*to Bob*) The other lady on her way up?
Bob Yes.
Tony (*to Mimi*) You're right—it's just beginning. I'm not staying to see it—I wanna live a bit longer.

Tony turns to go. Bob stops him

Bob Tony, please ...
Tony No—whatever it is, no!
Bob Look, Tony, you've got to help me. That's my wife coming up.
Tony I'm surprised you know who anybody is any more. I'm not even sure who *I* am. I certainly don't know who you are!
Bob I'm just a fellow human being in trouble. Now can you please delay that other lady for a little and give me time to do something with this one?
Tony What you gonna do with her?
Bob Get her out of here.
Mimi Who says?
Bob (*frantically*) Look don't you make things worse than they are already! (*Beseechingly*) Please, Tony.
Tony What am I gonna tell the other one this time? She up and down stairs like a yo-yo!
Bob What message did the other gentleman give her?
Tony He just say he wanna see her up here.

Bob Well say he now wants to see her down there.
Tony How can he? He next door.
Bob What's he doing there?
Tony Eating your steak.
Bob Who with?
Tony Your other lady.
Bob The swine!
Tony What's it matter to you? You got your hands full here.
Bob (*shouting at the connecting door*) Well tell him to leave that lady alone!
Tony Look I'm a waiter, not a pigeon service! Which one you want me to tell first?
Bob Er—the lady who's coming up. Tell her to go back down again.
Tony Down where?
Bob The restaurant. (*He brightens*) That's it! Tell her I—I mean he—will see her in the restaurant.
Tony And are you or he gonna see her?
Bob (*angrily*) I don't know! What does it matter who sees her? Just get rid of her for a while—then I'll deal with her.
Tony (*shouting back*) OK, OK! I'll tell her to go down again and wait for him who might be you who may or may not see her sooner or later down there or up here. I hope she knows what I'm talking about because I sure as hell don't!

Tony storms out, slamming the main door

Bob takes a deep breath and wipes his forehead

Bob These temperamental Italians! (*He turns to Mimi*) Now look, Mimi . . .
Mimi (*sweetly*) Yes?
Bob I don't know what Geoff Tippett's told you, or what his game is, but believe me I've got a problem.
Mimi So you said. (*She starts to unbutton her dress*) Let's see what we can do about it.
Bob (*hastily*) No, no—not that kind of problem! The problem is that I have ended up with three women on my hands all at once, one of whom happens to be my wife . . .
Mimi I thought you'd left your wife?
Bob Who told you that?
Mimi Geoff.
Bob Oh did he? Well why he's arranged for both you and my wife to be here on the same evening, I just . . . (*He stops thoughtfully*) Unless he didn't.
Mimi Well if he didn't, who did?
Bob (*shaking his head*) I don't know. I don't understand anything any more—I'm out of my depth. All I know is I wish I'd stayed at home and never got involved in any of it.
Mimi Stayed at home with your wife, you mean?
Bob Yes even that. I'm not cut out for the high life. Geoff Tippett can keep it!
Mimi What about the one next door?

Act II

Bob I wish I hadn't met her most of all. That's what really put the cat amongst the pigeons. I can't cope with a grand passion at my time of life.
Mimi All right, darlin', if that's how you feel. (*She gets off the bed*) I'll just go and tidy up, and then I'll be off.
Bob Off? You mean go?
Mimi (*sweetly*) That's right. Quick wash and brush up, and you'll never see me again.
Bob Oh thank you, thank you!
Mimi (*looking around*) Where's my bag?

Bob gets it out of the fridge and gives it to her

Bob Just keeping it fresh for you. I'll just make sure the coast is clear. (*He dashes to the main door, then turns and dashes back. He kisses her heartily*) I'll never forget this!

Bob dashes out to the corridor

Mimi You're dead right you won't. (*She takes off her sunglasses and her wig, and is revealed as Liz*)

She takes her things and vanishes into the bathroom. Bob dashes back in from the corridor

Bob It's all right—every ... (*He sees the room is empty and goes to the bathroom door. Calling urgently*) Don't be long! (*He wavers, then closes the main door, goes to the connecting door and knocks*)

Dick and Kate look at each other

Dick (*calling*) Who is it?
Bob Er—excuse me a moment, could I have a word with Kate?

Dick unlocks the door and peers through

Dick Are you alone?
Bob Yes.
Dick Where's Liz—I mean Mimi—I mean ...?
Bob They've both gone elsewhere for the moment.
Dick (*puzzled*) Both?
Bob Yes. Look I just want a quick word with Kate in private.
Dick I don't know that I'll allow that.
Bob (*angrily*) Don't start that again! It's for her to say, not you.
Dick (*turning to Kate*) Do you want a word with him in private?
Kate As long as he's certain who he is this time.
Dick (*to Bob*) Do you know who you are?
Bob Yes, yes—no more tricks I promise.

Dick stands aside, and Kate goes through

Dick If he tries anything funny just shout and I'll come and thump him.
Bob For a psychiatrist you're very unsubtle.
Dick For a Don Juan figure you're very inept! (*He shuts the door*)
Bob (*sadly*) Yes, he's right—I am.

Kate What's happened?
Bob Look, I just want you to know that I meant what I said before. You're the nicest thing that's happened to me for years, and if it was possible I'd like it to go on happening.
Kate But it's not possible?
Bob I don't know. My wife is down in the restaurant. I don't know why she's here or what she expects, but I'm going to go down and finally have everything out with her.
Kate In the middle of the restaurant? If it's anything like your previous attempts you'll both be thrown out on the street.
Bob It'll be quite civilized, I promise you. I just want you to give me a little more time to—to work things out.
Kate Very well.
Bob (*indicating next door*) You won't get involved with him meanwhile, will you?
Kate Why should I do that?
Bob Well the computer seems to think you're a good match for each other.
Kate Computers don't deal in chemistry.
Bob No.
Kate Could I have another kiss before you go?
Bob Ah ... er ... (*He glances quickly at the bathroom and the bedroom doors*) Why not?

They kiss. Both sigh, Bob opens the main door to leave

Kate I'll wait for you here. (*She reclines on the bed*)

Bob shuts the door again hurriedly

Bob (*anxiously*) Oh, er—I don't know that that's a very good idea.
Kate Why not?
Bob It's a bit public here.
Kate We can lock all the doors.
Bob But that's a bed.
Kate Yes.
Bob And we've both had a lot of champagne this evening.
Kate Yes.
Bob And you took great exception to both those items earlier.
Kate A lot's happened since then. As I told you, I'm very fond of champagne, and beds, under the right circumstances.
Bob Ah.
Kate It's up to you to get the circumstances right.
Bob (*wavering between the bed and the bathroom*) Well, er—that might take a little doing.

There is a knock on the main door

Oh no! (*To Kate*) I'm terribly sorry. (*He lifts the bed*)

Kate squeals and disappears into the alcove

Bob opens the main door

Act II

Tony stands there

(*Apoplectic; shouting*) What is it *this* time?
Tony (*shouting back*) Don't shout! I don't like shouting!
Bob (*still shouting*) What do you *want*?
Tony (*shouting*) I don't want anything! I just come to tell you something!
Bob (*shouting*) What? What?

Dick charges in, having heard the shouting

Dick (*shouting*) What is it? What's happening?
Bob (*shouting*) You keep out of this!
Dick (*shouting*) Don't shout at me like that!
Bob (*shouting*) It's none of your business—get back where you belong!
Tony (*shouting*) What you shouting at him for now?
Bob ⎫   ⎧ I'm not shouting, I'm just telling him to mind ...
Dick ⎬(*together*) ⎨ I'll do nothing of the sort until I know what's ...
Tony ⎭   ⎩ You crazy, all of you, crazy! I never met such ...
Bob (*roaring*) QUIET!

Silence

(*Hoarsely, to Dick*) Now please, can I ask you very politely to go back in there and leave us alone.
Dick Where's Kate?
Bob She's er—in the bathroom.
Tony With Mimi?
Dick (*frowning*) Mimi?
Bob (*almost on his knees*) Please ... please ...! I beg you—leave me alone to sort it all out.
Dick All right, but I'm warning you—this game has gone on long enough. This is your last chance, do you hear me? (*He returns to the R room and closes the connecting door*)

Bob breathes a sigh of relief

Dick thinks for a moment, picks up his umbrella, then goes out to the corridor, closing the door

Bob (*turning to Tony*) Now then, Tony?
Tony I just come to tell you that I can't find her.
Bob Find who?
Tony Who? Who you think—who? The lady you sent me to find—that's who! She not in the lift, she not in the restaurant, she not anywhere. She gone—sparito!
Bob (*despairingly*) Oh my God!
Tony (*looking around*) Where's Mimi?
Bob I told you, in the bathroom.

Again a muffled cry from the alcove. Tony stares

Tony I'm not gonna ask.
Bob (*going to the bed*) I'll show you. (*He starts to let the bed down*)

Liz (*off, calling from the bathroom*) Can I come out now?
Bob (*pushing the bed back*) Yes.

The bathroom door opens and Liz comes out wearing her own dress and carrying Mimi's bag

Both men stare in astonishment

Liz Hello, boys.
Bob (*speechless*) What...? Where...? How did you get in there?
Liz Through the door.
Bob Where's Mimi?
Liz Gone.
Bob Gone where?

She takes Mimi's wig from her bag and throws it to Bob

Liz Here.

Long pause

Bob It's not possible.
Liz Didn't know I was such a good actress, did you, darling?
Tony You mean there isn't a Mimi?

She shakes her head

There never was a Mimi?

She shakes again. Tony looks at Bob

Who is this lady—for true?
Bob I told you—my wife.
Tony And you didn't recognize her when she was Mimi?
Bob *You* didn't recognize her.
Tony (*demented*) She not my wife! You gotta chick in here, and you gonna go to bed with her, and she's your own wife, and you don't recognize her? You more crazy than I thought possible, and that's not possible!!
Liz He wasn't going to go to bed with her—luckily for him.

Bob collapses into the chair, stunned

Bob I'm never going to bed with anybody ever again. (*He turns back to her*) Where did you get that outfit?
Liz There's a little boutique in the foyer.
Bob What did you do it for?
Liz To test you—see if you'd go through with it.
Tony Ay, yi, yi. You had a close whisker there, signor.
Bob Who asked you?
Tony Sorry.
Bob (*to Liz*) Very clever.
Liz I can be sometimes.
Bob Oh you are. Far too clever for me.
Tony (*nodding*) Yeah.
Bob Quiet you!

Act II

Tony Sorry.
Liz Not cleverer—just better at disguises.
Bob Disguises?
Liz That ridiculous Indian get-up.
Bob Did you know that was me?
Liz Of course I knew it was you. Apart from anything I gave you that tie for Christmas. (*Pause*) What happened to it?
Bob (*looking down at it*) It's changed its religion.
Liz Anyway, I recognized all the polishing marks on it.
Tony Heh, heh, heh!
Bob I said quiet!
Tony Sorry.
Bob (*to Liz*) What are you doing here anyway?
Liz Geoff asked me out—to cheer me up supposedly.
Bob I see. So why were you having dinner with Dick the Shrink?
Liz There was no-one else. I was obviously meant to meet you but you'd gone off with Computer Kate. Anyway I thought you were supposed to be in Manchester.
Bob Only for the day. I came back on Tuesday.
Liz So you've been staying here since?
Bob No fear! I wouldn't stay anywhere that had him for room service.
Tony Thank you very much.
Bob I've been staying with Geoff.

Liz throws back her head and laughs

Liz And he told you he'd fixed a naughty night out with Mimi?
Bob (*uncomfortably*) Well—yes.
Liz As a present for your birthday no doubt.
Bob Well it was a better one than gardening gloves.
Liz While at the same time he was inviting me here for dinner with him.
Bob So it was all a scheme to get us together again.
Liz Looks like it.
Bob Dear old Geoff.
Liz Yes, dear old Geoff. Only you had to go and confuse matters.
Bob It wasn't my fault. (*He indicates Tony*) It was his.
Tony Mine?
Bob You let the wrong woman get in here.
Tony It was you told me to fix it so you could have dinner with her.
Liz I see—so you fell for her?
Bob Well, I . . .
Liz Did you, or didn't you?
Tony Yes, he did.
Bob Belt up, you!

Tony belts up

Liz All over one bottle of champagne. How naïve!
Bob Well if I'd had a better time of it with you these last few years I mightn't have been so wide open.
Liz Well you give me a better time and you might *get* a better time.

Bob What do you mean?
Liz Why don't you take *me* out for naughty nights in hotels once in a while—don't wait for Geoff to set them up for you. Open champagne bottles with me—don't waste them on Kates and Mimis.
Tony That's right.
Bob Look, do you want another eye-patch?
Tony Sorry.
Bob (*to Liz*) I didn't know that was what you wanted.
Liz Neither did I until I tasted it. But it's as clear as a bell now—that's what our marriage needs, adrenalin!
Bob Yes.
Liz Excitement!
Bob Quite.
Liz So excite me.
Tony Not in front of me, please. I'll leave you to it. I'll see you're not disturbed like you didn't wanna be disturbed the last time, and the time before that. (*At the door*) There's just one thing. (*He beckons Bob to him*)
Bob What?
Tony Don't excite her in the bed—you might find it a bit overcrowded.

Tony goes

Bob (*remembering*) Oh my God!
Liz What did he mean by that?
Bob I, er ... he, er ...
Liz Haven't arranged for Kate to come back again, have you?
Bob No, no, no ...
Liz Where is she by the way?
Bob Oh er—hanging about somewhere.
Liz Well I suggest you forget about her. Let's do as Geoff intended and start afresh. We've got a room to ourselves ... (*She picks up the brandy glass*) ... we've got brandy ... (*She goes towards the bed*) we've got a bed ...
Bob (*leaping to the bed and flattening himself against it*) No!
Liz What's the matter?
Bob I er—I've got a headache.
Liz What?
Bob I mean, let's work up to the bed gradually.
Liz (*sighing*) There you go again—everything by the book.
Bob I'm just afraid of being interrupted—there are so many people around. I know—why don't you pop next door to Dick, and tell him that Kate will be joining him shortly?
Liz Will she? How do you know?
Bob Well she's tied up elsewhere at the moment, but she'll soon be free. Then, when we know they're all right, we can relax and do whatever we want to do.
Liz (*approaching him*) Such as finish dinner?
Bob If you like.
Liz (*playing with his shirt buttons*) Have some more brandy?

Act II

Bob Yes.
Liz (*scratching his chest*) And let the bed down . . . ?
Bob (*fervently*) I sincerely hope so.
Liz Right. Don't go away.

He shakes his head dumbly. Liz goes through to the R *room. Bob starts to let the bed down*

   Dick enters the L *room from the corridor, still carrying his umbrella*

Bob pushes the bed back again

Dick (*belligerent with champagne*) All right, where is she?
Bob Who?
Dick Kate, that's who.
Bob What do you want to know for?
Dick I've decided the computer was right. She's my sort of girl.
Bob You've been chasing my wife all night!
Dick I never chased your wife. We were thrown together because of your infantile philanderings elsewhere.
Bob My *what*?
Dick All right, all right—I don't absolve myself completely, but it's now time for us all to reject our fantasizing impulses and adopt an objective attitude to the situation.
Bob What are you talking about?
Dick That's psychiatrist's jargon for let's come back to earth and stop arsing about. Where's Kate?
Bob That's not within the scope of your information entitlement.
Dick What?
Bob That's civil servant's jargon for none of your bloody business.
Dick Of course it's my business! Where . . . ? (*He notices the wig and picks it up curiously*)
Bob (*grabbing it from him*) That's none of your business either.
Dick Where is she?
Bob I'm not leaving her to a crackpot psychiatrist like you.
Dick I'll crack your pot in a minute!

Dick goes to hit him with his umbrella which promptly opens automatically above his head

   Bob takes advantage of the distraction to lock himself in the bathroom

Dick struggles to retract his umbrella. Next door, Liz has been looking for Dick in the bathroom without success

   Tony enters the R *room carrying a bill*

Tony Now, signor, I—— ahh! (*He sees Liz and does a smart "U" turn*)
Liz Tony——
Tony No, no, no!
Liz Tony, I just——
Tony I don't wanna know!

Tony goes out again

Dick succeeds in retracting his umbrella and starts thumping on the bathroom door with it as Liz comes back through the connecting door

Dick Come out of there!
Bob (*off, shouting back*) No!
Liz Oh—there you are.

Dick is caught with umbrella in mid-air

Dick (*foolishly*) Ah—hello.

Tony enters the L room

Tony (*as he enters*) Signor, I—— (*Seeing the others*) Ahhh!

Tony exits

Liz What are you doing?
Dick Er—trying to get your husband to come out of the bathroom.
Liz What's he doing in there?
Dick Refusing to tell me where Kate is.
Liz Why do you want to know?
Dick I think this has gone on long enough. I think it's time we all went right back to the beginning and did things as we were meant to do them in the first place.
Liz I agree.
Dick He doesn't.

She goes to the bathroom door and bangs on it

Liz Bob, come out of there!
Bob (*off, calling*) Not till that madman's left.
Liz Will you tell him where Kate is?
Bob (*off*) No!

There is a muffled cry from Kate

Kate (*off, from the alcove*) Dick!
Dick Yes?
Liz Pardon?
Dick I thought you said something.
Liz It was next door.

Tony enters the R room

Tony (*seeing the empty room*) Crazy! All crazy!

Dick goes through the connecting door

Dick Tony!
Tony (*jumping*) Ahh!
Dick Tony, I——
Tony No, no, no!
Dick I just wanted to ask a question.

Act II

Tony Look—I gotta bill here for a helluva lotta dinners and cognacs and coffees. Are you gonna pay it?
Dick Not just yet. We've more important things to sort out.
Tony For me that's the most important thing. I wanna get home and get to bed and forget all about you crazy people! Where the other guy?
Dick (*pointing next door*) Hiding in the bathroom.
Tony Ah. (*He goes through*)
Dick (*following*) Where's the other lady?
Tony Don't ask me. Last I saw she was hiding in the wall.
Dick (*puzzled*) In the wall?
Tony (*crossing to the bathroom*) Now she's probably in the fridge. (*He bangs on the door*) Signor—come outa there!
Bob (*off*) No!
Tony (*returning to the centre of the room*) Right—that's it! Nobody leaves this room. I gonna get the manager.

Tony exits

Another muffled cry from Kate

Kate (*off*) Let me out!
Dick ⎫ (*together to each other*) Pardon? (*They stare at each other, then at the*
Liz ⎭ *bed*)
Dick It came from there! (*He lets the bed down*)

An angry Kate appears

Stunned pause

Kate I feel like a squashed grape!
Dick What are you doing there?
Kate (*nodding at Liz*) Ask her husband. (*She gets off the bed and storms towards the bathroom*)
Dick Kate, I've been looking for you ...
Kate (*sweeping him aside like a piece of confetti*) I heard. (*She bangs on the bathroom door*) You, come out of there!
Bob (*off*) No!
Liz You mean he shut you up in the bed?
Kate Yes.
Liz Why?
Kate To hide me from you.
Liz (*going to the door and banging on it*) You, come out of there!
Bob (*off*) No!
Dick (*going to Kate*) Kate, forget him—he's a lost cause. Come with me.
Kate You're a lost cause.
Dick Not any more. I've made my decision and this time I'm going to stick to it.
Kate You couldn't stick to a lump of super-glue.
Dick (*bridling*) Oh no? We'll see about that. (*He grabs her by the arm*) Come with me.
Kate Where to?

Dick Somewhere quiet and peaceful where we can have a nice civilized meal and get to know each other properly.
Kate We've already had dinner and you don't like restaurants.
Dick I wasn't thinking of dinner or a restaurant.
Kate What were you thinking of?
Dick Breakfast at my place. (*He forcibly flings her through the door*)

Kate disappears with a squeal

(*He turns and grins at Liz, and flexes his shoulder muscles. In an Italian accent*) That's what you need with the chicks—a little macho, a little style. Arrivederci, baby!

Dick swaggers out of the door, swinging his umbrella

Liz (*banging on the bathroom door*) Bob, come out of there!
Bob (*off*) No!
Liz He's gone. She's gone. There's no-one left but me.

The bathroom door opens and Bob comes out wearing Mimi's wig and dress. He wiggles past Liz, who peals with laughter

Bob Sorry, sweetie—you're not my type.

Tony enters L room

Tony Now, the manager ... (*He sees Bob*) Mimi! (*His eyes light up, he pinches Bob's bottom and leads him out of the room*) Buona serra, baby!
Bob (*appealing back to Liz*) No, wait, no ...!

CURTAIN

FURNITURE AND PROPERTY LIST

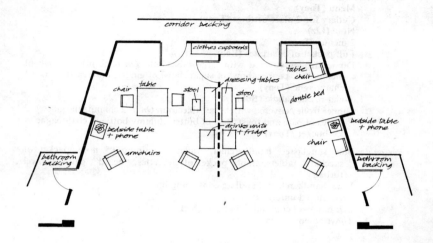

ACT I

On stage: R ROOM

    Table. *On it:* 2 dinner-place settings, 2 glasses, 2 menus
    2 chairs
    Fitted clothes cupboard. *In it:* hangers
    Dressing-table unit with mirror and stool
    Drinks unit with small fridge. *On top:* glasses, assorted selection of spirits in miniature bottles (including vodka) and soft drinks (including tonic water)
    2 armchairs
    Bedside table. *On it:* phone
    Concealed double bed (dummy) in alcove

L ROOM

    Pull-down double bed concealed in alcove. *On it:* pillows, bedclothes, bedspread
    Bedside table. *On it:* phone
    Table
    2 chairs
    Fitted clothes cupboard
    Dressing-table unit with mirror and stool

Birthday Suite

Drinks unit with small fridge. *On top:* glasses, assorted selection of spirits in miniature bottles (including Scotch and vodka) and soft drinks (including tonic water)
Ice-bucket containing ice and unopened bottle of champagne with napkin round neck
2 armchairs
Key in connecting door

Off stage: Small overnight bag **(Bob)**
Menu **(Tony)**
Cutlery for 2 place settings **(Tony)**
Note **(Liz)**
2 menus **(Tony)**
Full packet of cigarettes **(Bob)**
Dinner trolley covered with large tablecloth. *On it:* 2 plates, bowl of melon, salt, pepper, bowl of sugar, bowl of ginger, unopened bottle of champagne **(Tony)**
Toilet-brush handle **(Bob)**
Dinner trolley covered with large tablecloth. *On it:* 2 champagne glasses, 2 plates of pâté and toast, dish of butter, dummy bottle of champagne in ice-bucket **(Tony)**

Personal: **Bob:** sunglasses, handkerchief, wallet containing £5 note, packet of saccharin tablets, empty packet of cigarettes, "beard", padded towel turban
Kate: handkerchief, handbag containing lipstick
Dick: furled umbrella
Liz: handbag containing handkerchief
Tony: notepad, pen

ACT II

Strike: Dummy bottle of champagne from R room

Set: Unopened bottle of champagne in ice-bucket in R room

Re-set: 2 champagne glasses, 2 plates of pâté and toast, dish of butter, ice-bucket on the table

Check: Key in connecting door in L room

Off stage: Dinner trolley covered with large tablecloth. *On it:* 2 plates of shish kebab, bowl of salad (including an onion), salad servers **(Tony)**
Dinner trolley covered with large tablecloth. *On it:* 2 plates of fillet steak, bowl of salad **(Tony)**
Tray containing 2 coffee cups and saucers with spoons, pot of coffee, bowl of sugar, jug of cream etc. **(Tony)**
Tray containing 2 cognacs **(Tony)**
Bill **(Tony)**

Personal: **Bob:** beard
Tony: eye-patch
Mimi: bag, large sunglasses, wig
Dick: umbrella

LIGHTING PLOT

Property fittings required: nil
Interior. The same scene throughout

ACT I
To open: Full general lighting
No cues

ACT II
To open: Full general lighting
No cues

EFFECTS PLOT

ACT I

Cue 1   **Bob** sits on the end of the bed   (Page 30)
        Phone rings in L *room*